COGS AND MONSTERS

Cogs and Monsters

What Economics Is, and What It Should Be

Diane Coyle

PRINCETON UNIVERSITY PRESS

PRINCETON AND OXFORD

Published by Princeton University Press
41 William Street, Princeton, New Jersey 08540
99 Banbury Road, Oxford OX2 6JX

press.princeton.edu

All Rights Reserved

First paperback printing, 2023
Paperback ISBN 9780691231044

The Library of Congress has cataloged the cloth edition as follows:

Names: Coyle, Diane, author.
Title: Cogs and monsters : what economics is, and what it should be / Diane Coyle.
Description: Princeton : Princeton University Press, [2021] |
    Includes bibliographical references and index.
Identifiers: LCCN 2021017044 (print) | LCCN 2021017045 (ebook) |
    ISBN 9780691210599 (hardcover ; alk. paper) | ISBN 9780691231037 (ebook)
Subjects: LCSH: Electronic commerce—History—21st century. | Digital
    media—History—21st century. | Economics—History—21st century. |
    BISAC: BUSINESS & ECONOMICS / Economics / General |
    BUSINESS & ECONOMICS / Public Finance
Classification: LCC HF5548.32 .C69 2021 (print) | LCC
    HF5548.32 (ebook) | DDC 330—dc23
LC record available at https://lccn.loc.gov/2021017044
LC ebook record available at https://lccn.loc.gov/2021017045

British Library Cataloging-in-Publication Data is available

Editorial: Hannah Paul, Josh Drake
Production Editorial: Terri O'Prey
Jacket/Cover Design: Karl Spurzem
Production: Erin Suydam
Publicity: James Schneider, Kate Farquhar-Thomson

Jacket/Cover image by Ryger / Shutterstock

This book has been composed in Adobe Text and Gotham

Printed in the United States of America

Dedicated to the memory of Peter Sinclair,
1946–2020

CONTENTS

COGS AND MONSTERS

Introduction

ECONOMICS TODAY AND TOMORROW

Economics comes in for plenty of criticism. It is not hard to understand why, given that events like the 2008–2009 financial crisis, the Brexit vote in the UK, or even the rise of populism across the western democracies, seemed to catch the economics profession off-balance. Yet many criticisms of the subject long pre-date these specific events, while the substance of what most of them say has not changed since at least the early 2000s: economists make assumptions about people being selfish, calculating individuals; economics is all complicated mathematics and ignores the real world; economists only care about money and profit, not about truly valuable things like the environment. These are familiar accusations, given a new edge by events. Yet at the same time, economics has become more successful than ever in terms of its influence on policy-making, or more materially in terms of the incomes economics graduates can earn (Britton et al. 2020).

The unchanging critique is deeply frustrating to many of us in the economics profession because it sets up straw men, while ignoring deep-seated problems that are likely to present more significant challenges. Economics has changed a lot in recent decades. It needs to change a lot in future—but the critique needs to move on too, to address what really needs attention.

To take the issues with critique first, one of its standard elements is that economics uses abstract models written down in mathematical formulae. There is certainly abuse of mathematical formalism in economics (Romer 2015), but every discipline uses 'models' in the sense of selecting a small number of elements in the complex world to investigate causal relations. 'The causes of the first world war' is a model, just as much as Gary Becker's (1965) theory of time allocation.

Another common criticism is that economics ignores history, including its own history of thought. Many of us would love economic history to return to its former place as a standard part of the curriculum—a trend that has already started in many courses. So too has the teaching of the links between historical events, the history of economic ideas, and policy choices (something covered in Chapter Six). Research in economic history is thriving currently, albeit from a small base, and so too is institutional economics, for which understanding historical context is essential.

This criticism therefore has merit but those who deploy it are somewhat ahistorical themselves in refusing to recognise that the discipline has been changing dramatically during the past thirty years. There has been a substantial turn away from theory to empirical work (Angrist et al. 2017). Most economists do applied microeconomic research, where data sets, econometric techniques, computer power, and a lively methodological debate about causal inference mean there has been an effective revolution in knowledge and practice since the 1980s. Economics is at the forefront of using new massive data sets—'big data' (Athey 2017). None of the recent critics (such as Skidelsky 2020) acknowledge this. Indeed most critics only discuss macroeconomics (the study of the aggregate behaviour of the economy as a whole), which is an easy target because macroeconomic forecasting is genuinely difficult, far harder than weather forecasting.

A different type of criticism reflects mutually incompatible views about whether there can be advances in economic knowledge. Heterodox critics advocate pluralism in approaches to economics (for example, Earle, Moran, and Ward-Perkins 2016). They seem to see the subject as comparable to the humanities, where fundamental truths do not exist and ultimately researchers' values determine their conclusions. The main body of the economics profession—label it mainstream or neoclassical or even neoliberal—believes that knowledge about economics does accumulate (although none want economics to be just like physics, as some critics continue to claim; true in the 1950s or '60s perhaps, but not in the 2020s). All economists would agree that values and ideologies affect policy choices. Many think it possible nevertheless to separate empirical knowledge—how much is a higher tax rate likely to reduce demand for sugary drinks?—from political values—should the government protect consumers from their own bad choices?

To my mind, values cannot be wholly separable from empirical investigation, and yet it is important for economists to aspire to be as impartial as possible. Economic knowledge certainly accumulates. If we had not learned lessons from the experience of the 1930s, the consequences of the 2008–9 financial crisis would have been far more severe, and governments would not have introduced furlough schemes during the coronavirus lockdowns. If we had not created and learned from market design (defining the rules that make markets work well), far fewer of the apps on our phones could work.

There are other important differences between economics and its critics. One is whether it is ever acceptable to put monetary values on intrinsically good things like nature or human life. The economists' answer is that there are implicit valuations made whenever people make choices about where to build roads or what safety features to require of new products, so is it not better to be explicit about those judgements? These are healthy debates, generally with constructive mutual engagement among the participants. Indeed, some leading economists have begun to argue for a closer dialogue between economics and ethics (Bowles 2016), and to identify the importance of identity (Akerlof and Kranton 2010), and narrative and persuasion (Shiller 2019). This engagement with the humanities is necessary and welcome (Morson and Shapiro 2016).

A number of studies have also noted the (unmerited?) 'superiority' or 'imperialism' of economics or, in other words, economists' confidence that their approach is best when it comes to answering questions or addressing policy problems (for example, Fourcade, Ollion, and Algan 2015). This is slowly changing, albeit with further to go. One piece of evidence is the growing cross-citation among the social sciences (Angrist et al. 2020). Although it is still an unbalanced trade in the sense that economics is cited more by the other disciplines than vice versa, the trend is for more cross-fertilisation. Anybody supervising PhD students or mentoring younger colleagues will know about the geyser of interest in broad societal problems requiring interdisciplinary work across the natural and social sciences and the arts and humanities.

Another welcome change in recent years is the gathering pace of curriculum reform. As explained in the text, this was prompted by a combination of some effective student protests in countries from Chile to the UK about the inadequacy of their economics courses in teaching real-world issues with unease among university teachers and employers about what economics graduates had learned. I have been part of the coalition of economists around the world devising and making freely available a curriculum significantly different from the Economics 101 norm, changing the benchmark way of thinking about the world that students learn in what is often their first encounter with economics (Bowles and Carlin 2020). Many universities are adopting the new framework.

This book reflects my frustration with the straw men arguments because, as well as ignoring welcome changes in economics and in the way it is taught, they have allowed economists to overlook or deny some things that are badly wrong with the discipline, both in its intellectual approach and in the ways economists are so unrepresentative of the societies we aim to study.

In recent years, in a succession of public lectures, I have addressed some of these issues. Economists do not introspect much about deep methodological questions. The lectures on which this book builds had as one thread some key philosophical issues in economics itself: to what extent is economics performative, or self-fulfilling? Can a social science ever aspire to objectivity when its practitioners are part of society? What policy conclusions can we possibly draw from economics when it assumes people have fixed preferences—an assumption torpedoed by the existence of the advertising industry? Has methodological individualism run out of road as the structure of the economy shifts to activities involving ever greater externalities and non-linear dynamics? A second thread is that the way in which the economy is changing, particularly because of digitalisation, means that our analysis of it needs to change. These threads explain the title of this book, *Cogs and Monsters*: the cogs are the self-interested individuals assumed by mainstream economics, interacting as independent, calculating agents in defined contexts. The monsters are snowballing, socially-influenced, untethered phenomena of the digital economy, the uncharted territory where so much is still unknown (labelled 'Here be monsters', on mediaeval maps). In treating us all as cogs, economics is inadvertently creating monsters, emergent phenomena it does not have the tools to understand.

There are, though, yet more important criticisms of economics today, concerning the sociology and culture of the discipline, and its shocking lack of diversity (in a broad sense).

There is a persuasive body of knowledge about the importance of cognitive diversity in solving problems and running organisations (Page 2007). Many of us now live in societies that are more diverse than in the past in terms of backgrounds and experiences. Diversity of experience matters in any social science because the questions researchers even think to ask are shaped by their own experience: you don't know what you don't know, and most of us are not able to imagine the shape of that unknown territory.

Economics stands out as one of the least diverse disciplines, even as it wields great practical influence, particularly over government policies that affect everyone in society. The subject's gender and ethnicity record is unacceptable. Economics is one of the most male-biased academic disciplines (Ceci et al. 2014). Although this has improved in US academia, just 14.5 percent of full professors were female in 2019, and 21.2 percent of all tenure-track academics; cold comfort that the former figure has doubled since 1994. The pipeline shrinks at each career stage, with 33.5 percent of economics undergraduate majors being female, and 32.2 percent of PhD students.[1] For the UK, against a background of improvement over a 20-year period, 20 percent of the academic workforce was female by 2016, but just 16.6 percent of full professors (Sevilla and Smith 2020). A recent study of European departments based on web-scraped data (rather than surveys) found that the representation of women falls from about 40 percent at the entry level to 22 percent among full professors (Auriol et al. 2020). There is additionally a lack of ethnic and cultural diversity in economics, although fewer survey results are available. One US study found that in 2015–2016 15.6 percent of economics degrees were awarded to members of minority groups.[2] In the UK in 1999 the figure was 12 percent (Blackaby and Frank 2000); absent later data, experience suggests it has changed little since then. Social class is less well measured still, but it is likely that the social experience of economics students in the UK at least has been getting narrower because an increasing proportion of its undergraduate students attend private schools. In contrast to some other disciplines, including many of the natural sciences, there has been little improvement in diversity in economics.

There is now a growing body of research showing that female economists are at a disadvantage. We publish less than male economists on average, and female-authored papers at some elite journals are subjected to extended review times (Hengel 2020). Card et al. (2020, 14) write: 'Editors appear to be gender-neutral in the value they place on the recommendations of male

---

1. Committee on the Status of Women in the Economics Profession Annual Report 2019, https://www.aeaweb.org/content/file?id=11630.

2. Report of the Committee on the Status of Minority Groups in the Economics Profession (CSMGEP) December 2017, https://www.aeaweb.org/content/file?id=6592.

and female referees. . . . However, all referees appear to hold female-authored papers to a higher bar than male-authored papers, if we measure paper quality by citations. All-female-authored papers receive about 25 percent more citations than similar male-authored papers.' Women work on average with smaller networks of co-authors, which also tends to result in fewer publications (Ductor, Goyal, and Prummer 2020). The evidence for cumulative career disadvantage is powerful.

This lack of diversity matters for several reasons. One consequence is that academic economics in particular has a more aggressive culture than most other disciplines—reinforcing the gender bias in the profession. Any of us attending economics seminars will have experienced the frequent, challenging interruptions of speakers right from the start, making it impossible for them to present their work and get a constructive discussion, and silencing many voices in the room. Women presenters in seminars are asked more questions, and more that are perceived as unfair, than do men (Modestino et al. 2020). This alpha male, aggressive culture spills over into unacceptable behaviour more widely: Alice Wu made global headlines with her study of the macho, misogynist website Economics Job Market Rumors (Wu 2018). Other female economists and economists of colour have widely reported experiences ranging from constantly being patronised to outright harassment (for example, Sahm 2020).

Furthermore, the male domination of economics seems to shape the intellectual character of the discipline in ways that are unhealthy for a social science with so much influence on policy and society. The narrow frame of reference due in part to a limited range of life experiences shapes economists' ideas about which research questions are important and interesting. These ideas, and what gets researched, determine government policies, which in turn affect people's lives and choices. Yet women and people of colour will generally have different experiences, challenges, and priorities than affluent white men. More subtly, the values of economists and those of the population as a whole seem to diverge. Surveys show wide gaps between economists' views and public opinion on a range of policy questions, including politically contentious ones (e.g., Johnston and Ballard 2016). Economists have been found to be more individualist and even to be less pro-social than their peers (Bauman and Rose 2011; Frank, Gilovich, and Regan 1993), with some debate as to whether these types of people self-select into economics or whether learning the subject makes them this way.

The #metoo and #BlackLivesMatter movements have had an impact here as elsewhere. Professional organisations including the American Economic Association and the Royal Economic Society have responded to the lack of diversity and inclusivity in just the last two years or so. Their initial focus has been on gender and ethnicity. Change is clearly intended, with campaigns to attract students from a wider range of backgrounds,[3] new mentoring programmes, codes of conduct,[4] and above all much discussion and a growing awareness of the cultural and intellectual issues among the largely middle-class white male profession. How far this reaches inside the discipline is another matter: changes in social norms always take some time. Powerful male elites in top-rank American universities, gatekeepers to publication in the 'Top Five' journals necessary for good jobs and promotion, are adept at self-perpetuation.

3. Arun Advani, Rachel Griffith, and Sarah Smith, 'Economics in the UK Has a Diversity Problem That Starts in Schools and Colleges', https://voxeu.org/article/increasing-diversity-uk-economics.

4. American Economic Association, 'AEA Code of Professional Conduct', https://www.aeaweb.org/about-aea/code-of-conduct.

Economics still needs to confront these questions, ranging from the social make-up of the profession to its substantive intellectual content. I care deeply about these;[5] but this book reflects on the broader character of economics, not only its lack of inclusivity, and how the subject needs to change to be relevant for the rest of the twenty-first century. The issues covered here concern the fundamental paradigm—the subject's philosophical roots in utilitarianism, the validity of the distinction between positive and normative economics, the character of dynamic socio-economic systems that do not conform to the standard assumptions, the role of social influence in a discipline built on methodological individualism, and the scope for a powerful social science to alter its own subjects of study.

Although building on a number of public lectures given between 2012 and 2020, the material has been updated and set in a narrative arc illustrating the significant changes in economics that have occurred during the past decade. The book is aimed at general readers, not just economists. This is not only to focus attention on real challenges for economics rather than the straw man critiques, but also because the public appetite to understand the economy is intense. This is an extraordinary time in world history. The coronavirus pandemic means that people in every country have been experiencing an unprecedented economic shock, more sudden and severe than the Great Depression. It has galvanised the economics community, prompting a vast amount of new research and policy analysis, and stimulating many economists to engage with epidemiology and the biomedical sciences (Coyle 2020a). I

5. 'Women and Economics: Sixth 2018 Coleridge Lecture', https://www.ideasfestival .co.uk/blog/coleridge-lectures/coleridge-lecture-women-and-economics/, accessed 2 August 2020.

have been closely involved in this effort in the UK, particularly in the creation of an online observatory, ECO, synthesising the state of knowledge about the crisis.[6] Economics has a lot to offer in insight and advice to the policy-makers grappling with immense societal problems—not just the pandemic and its aftermath but also global environmental emergencies, and slow growth in economic opportunities along with unsustainable inequalities. This is the moment for economics to rise to the challenges set out here.

The book begins with the questions raised by the 2008–9 financial crisis. Chapter One explores the extent to which economics—specifically financial economics in this case— actually shapes the world rather than just analysing it. In other social sciences this phenomenon is called performativity. It is not unrelated to the more widespread notion of 'reflexivity' or the feedback between causal actor and effect. Many economists argue that economics played only a minor role in the crisis, upstaged by greed, or bad regulation. This is not the perception of non-economists, who also question why so few economists— with notable exceptions—predicted the crisis. Many critics do believe economics has shaped our societies for the worse, and whether you agree with them or not, this question should be confronted. The chapter puts the question of the responsibility of economics for events (in part I) in the context of the responsibilities of economics given the increasingly powerful role of economics in public policy (in part II). Even if you do not think economics is in any way performative, the latter responsibilities need to be taken more seriously than ever in an era when expertise is doubted or challenged. Economics is really once again political economy, just as it used to be known.

6. www.economicsobservatory.com/.

Chapter Two amplifies the theme of how hard it is to analyse the society you are part of, looking particularly at macroeconomics—the study of the economy as a whole, the behaviour of inflation, unemployment, interest rates, and growth. It was more justifiable to criticise macroeconomics in 2012 than it is now. There has been substantial subsequent change, prompted by the shock of the financial crisis. While there has undoubtedly been significant progress, my doubts about macroeconomics—unpopular among many colleagues—remain, for reasons explained here. In the public mind, too, it is macroeconomists who represent the technocratic elite.

The book then turns to the areas that are the bread and butter for a majority of economists, whether in the academic world or in policy, namely applied microeconomics. Most of us do not do macroeconomic forecasting, high profile as it is. Rather we are concerned with specific areas such as how competition in the food retailing industry works, what the effects of specific tax or benefit changes will be, which policy interventions will do most to help children struggling at school get better grades and life opportunities, or how firms learn about new production technologies and what makes them invest. The aim is often to figure out whether there is a better way of doing things in the specific context. Chapter Three questions some standard presumptions about what we take to be 'better', concerning assumptions we make about the way individuals take decisions, our own role as analysts of society in trying to change society—not only whether objectivity is possible (or do our own values always come into play?) but also what it means for things to be getting better? What does 'better' mean and for whom?

Chapter Four extends this to a world where policy decisions are increasingly being taken algorithmically, by machine learning systems which are programmed to decide as we economists

assume individuals decide: by seeking the best possible outcome for ourselves individually, on a well-specified definition
of 'best'. Machine learning systems are being created in the
image of the famous (or notorious) *homo economicus*, the calculating, self-interested individual. The chapter introduces the
question of data—the facts we think we know in analysing the
economy or making policy decisions. In the world of artificial
intelligence, the evident problems of data bias mean people are
becoming well aware that available data sets are in no way an
objective picture of society but rather a portrait that is painted
by society, its power structures and classifications. Although
economists are big users of data, including big data, paying
impressively careful attention to questions of causality and bias
in data samples, fewer have thought about the construction of
the data they use. My preoccupation has largely been macroeconomic data, and the fact that the variables we read about
in the news all the time—GDP and inflation—are ideas. We can
try to measure these concepts more accurately, for sure, but they
are not natural objects in the world. The same is true of many
of the constructs in empirical social science.

The final two chapters pull together the threads—do we
shape the society we analyse, can we hope to be objective, what
do we mean by economic progress or policies making things
'better', is the individualism we assume valid?—in the context
of the digital, twenty-first-century economy. Chapter Five concerns the economic analysis and Chapter Six the implications
for policy applications. I argue here that the ways technology
is changing the economy make these questions more acute. It
is becoming harder to understand from existing data whether
or not there is economic progress when the available statistics
present a fixed portrait of a changing landscape—as if maps
were trying to measure the depth of a river in its old location

when it has actually changed its course. But the more fundamental point is that the question of economic progress needs addressing in a different way to take account of the way the digital economy has been increasing our inter-relatedness (so individualism is ever less appropriate) and has different economic characteristics from the pre-digital economy.

This Introduction ends on a personal note. One of the early UK victims of Covid19 was Peter Sinclair, Professor of Economics at the University of Birmingham. He was my undergraduate tutor at Brasenose College, Oxford, whose enthusiasm and commitment to teaching turned me into an economist, and whose wisdom, concern for others, engagement with practical policy challenges, and range of knowledge made me the particular kind of economist I became. His widow, Jayne, found among the belongings returned to her by the hospital some notes he had scribbled before he lost consciousness. They seemed to be his thoughts about how to bring about an economic recovery from this crisis. We will have to recover without him, without the many other victims of the pandemic, which has taken such a terrible human toll. It is the responsibility of economists to ensure we contribute as best we can to the needed rebuilding.

1

The Public Responsibilities of the Economist

My 2007 book *The Soulful Science: What Economists Really Do and Why It Matters* was born of my frustration with the kind of straw man criticisms of economics described in the Introduction. Some of those criticisms—the overuse and abuse of mathematics, the extreme assumptions about rational, individual choice, abstractness from the real world, the merits of markets over government intervention—had been truer in 1985 than in 2005, when frustration drove me to the keyboard to start writing. The critics were ignoring the fact that economics had changed a lot in two decades.

I knew this because I had lived it. The period from 1981 to 1985 when I did my PhD at Harvard was the high-water mark in the academic profession of what might now be described as neoliberal economics. These were the Reagan and Thatcher years, both of whom were elected in reaction to the shortcomings of economic management by the state during the crises of the previous decade. I was as swayed by the intellectual tides as any other eager young economist, impressed by those who could wield the algebra and calculus more adeptly than I, and inclined to give market solutions to problems the benefit of the doubt. Still, my good luck with my teachers and mentors—Peter Sinclair at Oxford, Ben Friedman at Harvard—meant I was somewhat inoculated against the extremes of the 'rational expectations revolution'. It was also still the case then that the Harvard economics department required its graduate students to take two economic history courses along with the usual micro and macro theory and econometrics. In another stroke of luck my professors of these courses were the economic historian Barry Eichengreen and the heterodox economist Steve Marglin. While I rather naïvely disagreed with the latter, who was out of tune with the intellectual tides in Reagan's America, the readings and discussions certainly made me think.

In 1985, though, when I started my first job back in the UK as an economist at the Treasury, I would have defended the kind of economics most deserving of the frequent criticisms. Indeed, my job, in the grand Whitehall building just across the square from Parliament, was in the division responsible for monetary policy (this was before the days of central bank independence). The monetarism originating with Milton Friedman's work in the 1960s and implemented during the inflationary economic crises of the 1970s was the policy orthodoxy. We were also closely involved in the preparations for 'Big Bang', the removal of long-standing regulations governing the financial markets in the City of London. These 1986 deregulatory changes gave birth to the financial system that eventually delivered the Great Financial Crisis (GFC) of 2008–9, including the explosive growth of derivatives markets. (One of my tasks in the Treasury was writing an explainer about derivatives for senior officials and ministers, which was certainly an education for me too.)

By 2005, the orthodoxy had changed substantially—at least in the academic world. *The Soulful Science* is a description of what had changed. For example, the intervening twenty years had seen the introduction of endogenous growth theory (Romer 1986a), which linked economic growth to education and intellectual property rather than taking it as due to unexplained technical progress; and a broad appreciation of the role of institutions, or in other words historical and political context, in growth and in economic development (Acemoglu and Robinson 2012). Importantly, a constellation of computer power, new data sources, and improved statistical techniques had made empirical work both easier and more widespread. What *The Soulful Science* omitted—reflecting my own gaps in knowledge—was finance.

Of course, soon after the book was published, the GFC happened, taking the financial system literally to the brink of collapse, and causing a significant recession. This was not as bad as it might have been, as economists had learned from the 1930s—and one expert on the Great Depression, Ben Bernanke, was in a key role as chairman of the US Federal Reserve Board. Yet how had this cataclysmic event happened, after a long period some people had taken to calling the Great Moderation, with low inflation and steady growth? Her Majesty the Queen famously asked a group of economists at the London School of Economics why on earth they had not seen it coming. Macroeconomists were widely condemned for not having forecast the crisis, for many of the models used for forecasting at that time ruled out such events. Financial economists were mocked for their 'efficient markets hypothesis', the claim that asset prices captured all currently known information about future returns, so that their future movements could only be random.

Needless to say, I revised *Soulful* to acknowledge these short-comings (Coyle 2010). But the GFC has cast a long shadow. We have been living with its consequences ever since, particularly the way central banks' use of 'quantitative easing'—buying (mainly) government bonds to put money into the economy—has kept interest rates ultra-low, pumped up other asset prices to the delight of financial markets and rich asset owners, and plunged many pension funds into crisis. Having started ruminating on the role of finance and on the culpability of policy mistakes for what had happened, this became my subject when I was invited to give the 2012 Tanner Lectures on Human Values in Oxford.[1] What was the role of academic economics in creating and unleashing Frankenfinance—could its ideas have given birth to the monster? What were the responsibilities of policy economists, who had grown increasingly powerful in government since the mid-twentieth century, in allowing the financial crisis to happen? How should they apply economic research when faced with the roughness and messy complexity of the real world? Economics has moved on since 2012, but can we be sure something similar could never happen again?

Part I: Dr Frankenstein, I Presume?

These days, the most common question I get from junior analysts about derivatives is, 'How much money did we make off the client?' I attend derivatives sales meetings where not one single minute is spent asking questions about how we can help clients. It's purely about how we can make the most possible money off of them. It astounds me how little senior management gets a basic

1. https://www.bnc.ox.ac.uk/about-brasenose/news/982-tanner-lectures-2012.

truth: If clients don't trust you they will eventually stop doing business with you (Smith 2012).

These words, written in the *New York Times* by a departing Goldman Sachs executive a few years after the GFC, confirmed what many people believed then and still believe to be true about the financial markets. These markets are widely seen as having become fundamentally harmful to society. So too, by extension, are all markets and economists in general, since they are the principal advocates of markets as the organising structure of modern society. While this is perhaps an exaggeration of popular views, evidence from opinion surveys suggests there has been a reappraisal of the pro-market philosophy dominant in public policy since the early 1980s. Although majority public opinion continues to support a market-based economy, there is little popular enthusiasm for how the players in these markets have been behaving (YouGov 2011). Thanks to them, capitalism in the early twenty-first century has brought inequality, unemployment or precarious jobs, and austerity. Public dissatisfaction was strong enough by 2012 to get a fair number of people out onto the streets to 'Occupy' the commanding heights of the global economy in the City of London and on Wall Street. In 2019 polling in the United States by RealClear Opinion found more than a quarter of respondents saying capitalism and free markets are broken and another 15 percent saying they would like more government regulation of the economy.[2] Liberal intellectual opinion has been shrill in its denunciations of economics. Here is one example, from the American novelist Marilynne Robinson:

---

2. RealClear Opinion Research, https://www.realclearpolitics.com/docs/190305_RCOR_Topline_V2.pdf.

It is this supranational power, Economics Pantocrator, that failed us all in fairly recent memory. It has emerged from the ashes with its power and its prestige enhanced even beyond the status it enjoyed in the days of the great bubble. The instability and the destruction of wealth for which it is responsible actually lend new urgency to its behests (Robinson 2012).

She is not alone in regarding economics as a malign social force, rather than a useful practical discipline. There is a long tradition of writers seeing economics as conflicting with more important values or cultural traditions. It dates back to the Romantic backlash against the rationalist Enlightenment view of improvable Nature (Porter 2000). John Ruskin (1860) would have approved of Robinson's rant (there is no other word for it), having fulminated against industrial capitalism in a similar way in *Unto This Last*: whereas craft production created wealth, modern economics spawned 'illth', he claimed.

It is no surprise that what was then the deepest and longest economic downturn since the Great Depression—the pandemic probably will not take that title now—encouraged a revival of such criticism. If economists are supposed to help prevent or alleviate economic crises, it showed we have obviously not done a good job. While plenty of economists insist there is no fundamental problem with the subject, and many more would reject hyperbolic attacks from novelists and protestors, many others have been reflecting seriously on the lessons of the crisis for their intellectual framework and for the practical role they play in the world of public policy. Keynes famously said economists should be 'humble, competent people' like dentists, fixing things that go wrong and making modest improvements in people's lives (Keynes 1931). Esther Duflo, a recent

Nobel Laureate, opted instead for a comparison with plumbers, another practical profession (Duflo 2017).

Instead we have turned out to look more like Dr Franken-stein, unleashing an idealistic experiment that has run monstrously amok, causing devastation. Have economists created a monster? Has economics shaped the world in its own dysfunctional image?

There is some truth in this, in my view, when you get beyond the literary exaggerations. My profession does bear some responsibility for what has happened, in a way I will explain. But it is most true of a particular approach to economics, which has been retreating for some time and will eventually turn out to have been finally discredited by the GFC. The economic catastrophe could indeed be the making of a stronger economic science, re-rooted in the natural sciences, as it was at its birth in the Enlightenment. In the second part of this chapter, I will discuss how the struggle between old and new economics is playing out in the arena of public policy, where economists have for decades had a privileged status in influencing decisions.

This is my claim: economics as an intellectual discipline and professional practice has helped shape the economy it analyses. Beliefs about the way the economy works and expectations about how it will work in the future have a central role in our theories, or 'models'. In particular, many models—summaries of the relationships in the economy as a whole in the case of macroeconomics, or of a subset—assume that 'agents' (as we refer to people) have more or less correct beliefs or 'rational expectations' about the economy. At one level this is a reasonable assumption that you can't fool all of the people all of the time: if they are systematically proven wrong, they will change their beliefs. In practice, it becomes a strong—unrealistic—assumption about the information and powers of calculation of millions of real people.

However, the key point about the assumption that behaviour today depends on beliefs about tomorrow in any way, rational or not, is that it opens the door to self-fulfilling outcomes. Whenever expectations matter, ideas have the power to shape reality. Keynes's insistence on the importance of 'animal spirits' for investment and consumer spending is captured and pinned down in these formal rational expectations models, albeit not in a way he might have anticipated (Keynes 1936). Even speculative asset price bubbles can be rational in this sense: as long as most investors expect the price to continue rising, it will do so (Santos and Woodford 1997).

Economics owes the terminology of the self-fulfilling outcome to the sociologist Robert K. Merton, although there are many examples of the idea to be found before he coined the phrase (Merton and Merton 1968). One classical self-fulfilling prophecy is found in the Oedipal myth; the protagonists' expectations shaped by the prophecy are what bring about the very tragedy it foretells. As soon as the formal economic models that were developed from the late 1970s onwards incorporated a central role for expectations in decisions, almost everything could become self-fulfilling—indeed, instantaneously so in economists' unearthly world of perfect information and no frictions.

However, economists have never given much thought to the theoretical possibility this opens up, namely that the way economists think about the economy can become self-fulfilling too, that the principle works outside the models as well as inside them. If mainstream global economics models the economy or the financial markets in a certain way, and that enters the thoughts of public officials or financial market traders and shapes their beliefs and expectations, could reality change to reflect the model? If economists reflect a narrow slice of society and think in a distinctive way—and we are as a group demonstrated to be more selfish and individualist than average (Gerlach 2017)—then perhaps the models we use can shape the economy in the image conceived by the model-makers.

This is the strong version of self-fulfilling prophecy. It is often described as 'performativity', although this usage has travelled some distance from the word's origins in linguistic philosophy. John Austin used it for statements such as 'Sorry!' or 'I now pronounce you husband and wife,' in which the words themselves form the action (Austin 1962). Economic sociologists now use it for economic models that build their own reality, rather than merely describing an external reality. The canonical example of performative economics is the model for pricing financial options. Robert K. Merton's son, Robert C. Merton, was jointly awarded the Nobel Memorial Prize in Economics in 1997 for devising this model (along with Myron Scholes; Fisher Black, the other co-author of the original Black-Scholes model, had died earlier).[3] The investment company Robert C. Merton co-founded to put the model into practice, Long Term Capital Management (LTCM), went bankrupt with losses of $4.6 billion in 2000, in a kind of trial run for the later financial crisis. It is hard not to see some strange echo of the Oedipal story in this, especially as his father Robert K. is rumoured to have invested in LTCM.

How did the options pricing model of Merton *fils* alter financial reality in its own image, ultimately helping to bring about his catastrophic financial downfall? Sociologist Donald MacKenzie has traced the massive growth of derivatives markets since the 1970s to the availability of a practical model for

---

3. The Nobel Prize, https://www.nobelprize.org/prizes/economic-sciences/1997/advanced-information/.

pricing these financial instruments. Merton's contribution was to provide a simple version of the pricing formula for options, one that was more intuitive for traders in the markets than competing approaches because it related the option price to the volatility of the price of the underlying asset from which it was derived. What's more, as MacKenzie (2007) describes, Fisher Black also provided a commercial service to the financial markets in Chicago (at that time open outcry markets with traders shouting their deals in the various pits). His business calculated various options prices using the Black-Scholes-Merton model on computers away from the market and circulated them as single sheets of paper that a trader could roll up into a cylinder for ease of reading a specific column.

MacKenzie presents evidence that over a few years options prices observed in the US financial markets converged to those predicted by the model, the discrepancies between the model and the reality shrinking decade by decade as an ever-larger proportion of traders in the market used the same model for pricing their transactions. He also argues that the intellectual status of an economic theory born in the University of Chicago helped encourage the regulatory authorities not to ban options trading as a form of gambling. The combination of a trader-friendly model (subsequently greatly extended as the computer revolution made it easier for others to calculate prices according to the model), the successful commercial provision of pricing sheets, and sympathetic regulators brought into being a global derivatives market that grew from almost nothing in 1970 to a notional value of $1,200 trillion by 2010 (Triennial Central Bank Survey 2010).[4]

4. According to the most recent data from the Bank for International Settlements (BIS), the total notional amount outstanding for contracts in the over-the-counter

There is clearly more to this story than the intellectual act of creating and publishing an economic model. The wider sociology of the Chicago exchanges and the political environment of a less restrictive regulatory culture certainly played a part, as did the availability of computers and software to handle massive amounts of data and number-crunching. Nothing in the economy ever has a single cause. However, the argument that the Black-Scholes-Merton model played the Dr Frankenstein role in creating the dangerous monster of modern derivatives markets seems quite strong.

There is some reason to believe that the monster is still running amok in the financial markets, thanks to 'algos' (short for algorithm) carrying out ultra-high-frequency trading (HFT). Ultra-high frequency means transactions at intervals of 650 milliseconds or less. This activity has a cluster of support services such as businesses selling 'the fastest machine-readable economic data and corporate news', and 'global proximity hosting'.

The latter term refers to traders' need to locate their computer servers close to the computer servers of the exchanges on which they are trading. The reason is that at a nano-second (millionth of a millisecond) timescale, the speed of light becomes an important physical obstacle. Having to send instructions down a longer fibre-optic cable than a rival, taking nano-seconds longer, could be a costly disadvantage. The financial markets have gone through a phase of immaterial location in cyberspace and out the other side back into physical geography. New cables have been drilled through a corner of the Allegheny Mountains of Pennsylvania to bring Nasdaq's servers in Carteret, New Jersey,

---

derivatives market was about $560 trillion at the end of 2019. This is not directly comparable to the figure above, but there has been shrinkage during the past decade.

a little bit closer—three milliseconds to be exact—to photons originating in a data centre in Chicago's South Loop. A new trans-Atlantic cable has reduced transaction times by 0.006 of a second, an improvement well worth the $300 million investment. And in the anonymous-looking data centres, those servers located closest to the exchange's server are linked to it with redundant loops of fibre-optic cable so as to level the playing field with their electronic rivals a few metres further away. By 2017, the fastest possible response time between issuing and executing an order had dropped to 84 nano-seconds, 60 times faster than in 2011. The technology is going beyond cables. Rival networks of microwave towers have been built across Europe and within the United States, as over long distances microwaves can get closer than fibre-optic cables to speed-of-light transmission of data (Anthony 2016). Here are examples of the financial markets changing physical reality to carry out virtual, algebraic trades; of the markets literally moving mountains. A bid to build 300-metre-high microwave towers on England's lovely Kent coast—about the same height as New York's Chrysler Building—was rejected by the local council, however (Mackenzie 2019). New shortwave and satellite technologies are being developed. With about half the trades on financial markets now computerised HFT, this latest development conjures up the image of an algorithmic web of signals bouncing off low-earth orbit satellites, all for the financial markets to make more money faster off their clients.

There is evidence that the so-called flash crash of 6 May 2010, when the Dow Jones share price index fell 600 points in 6 minutes only to recover fully 20 minutes later, was due to automated trading of this kind. In 2015 the US authorities tried to pin the blame on a solo mathematically-gifted day trader, based in suburban West London, but as a recent account details, the crash was not the work of a human mastermind but rather of a complex network of machines and regulation (Vaughan 2020). Robinhood, the retail trading platform driving much of the Gamestop phenomenon in early 2021, was running orders through Citadel, an HFT trader that paid for those retail orders so it could glean intelligence about market conditions to give its own algorithms an advantage (Van Doren 2021).

The Gamestop rise and fall was all too obvious, but there is some evidence that there are very many flash crashes—more than 18,500 in the five years to 2011—too fast for humans to notice them (Johnson et al. 2012). In a report on this research, John Cartlidge of the University of Bristol, was quoted as saying: 'Economic theory has always lagged behind economic reality, but now the speed of technological change is widening that gap at an exponential rate. The scary result of this is that we now live in a world dominated by a global financial market of which we have virtually no sound theoretical understanding' (Keim 2012). Perhaps scarier, though, is the thought that economic theory is also ahead of economic reality, and there is no sound understanding of either. No wonder the novelist Robert Harris made an algorithm the rogue trader and central villain in his 2011 novel, *The Fear Index*. It is not clear whether it is reassuring or alarming that global financial regulators are clearly working hard on trying to understand what is happening in the financial markets, including their own role in creating dangerous complexity (Haldane 2012; Amadxarif et al. 2019).[5]

It seems unarguable that the financial markets have taken on a life of their own in our economies, powered by technology

---

5. Since then, there have been several reports and changes to legislation on the part of US regulators, while in European markets, the Market Abuse Regulation (MAR) came into force on 3 July 2016.

and, increasingly, AI. As one professional investor put it: "The ages-old fear of machines breaking away from their human masters to create their own civilization has been somewhat realized by a banking system that no longer exists to service the real economy" (Snider 2011). He described how just one bank, Bank of America, had a balance sheet exposure to $74 trillion of derivatives in the first nine months of 2011, although accountancy rules allow this to be presented as just $79 billion.[6]

Needless to say, none of this derivatives activity translates into investment in the real economy. The financial sector as a whole looks as though it contributes to growth in gross domestic product (GDP) only because of the way its activity has been defined and measured, known as FISIM—financial intermediation services indirectly measured. The definition in effect counts the risk-taking as a plus for the economy, speculative trading as well as potentially productive investment (Christophers 2013; Coyle 2014).

The possibility that the intellectual approach to finance prevailing since the 1970s has contributed little to the economy, and may indeed have subtracted value, raises some challenging questions. What should economists have done differently? Surely no regulator should have banned Professors Black, Scholes, and Merton from their research? Why has financial innovation proven so unrewarding for consumers, when innovation in every other sector of the economy generally benefits them, at least ultimately? These questions underline the fact that ideas do not live in a vacuum, but are embedded in institutional and social structures. For example, the benefits of innovation are usually spread through competition, whereas in finance there

6. According to the OCC, as of 31 December 2018 Bank of America still had $31.7 trillion in notional derivatives.

has been enough market power for financiers to extract mono-poly 'rents', or excess profits. Moreover, financial innovation left effective regulation behind, allowing greed, fraud, reckless-ness and overconfidence to run unchecked (Lanchester 2010).

MONSTERS AND MARKETS

Important as they are, culpable as they were in causing the GFC, financial markets are not the whole of the economy, nor is the Efficient Markets Hypothesis the whole of economics. The computers trading in financial markets are not economists, or embodiments of economics. Most economists would certainly not regard finance theory and the Efficient Markets Hypothesis as the pinnacle of their subject, to say the least. Politicians and regulators could tackle out-of-control financial markets with no violence to economics, if they wanted to.

So a number of economists have objected to my sugges-tion that the excesses of the financial markets have anything to do with economics at all. After all, many economists were in fact warning of unsustainable asset bubbles in the run-up to the crash (albeit that few specifically predicted a major banking crisis). Robert Shiller's *Irrational Exuberance* (2000) was a bestseller, and its warning featured widely in the media around the world. It is correct therefore to argue that political philosophy, the power of financial institutions, their lobbying of government, the incentives of credit rating agencies, and sheer greed and dishonesty all bear much greater responsibil-ity than economics, or even than options markets. If politi-cians and regulators had really been listening to economists, the crisis might have been averted. There is also a good case to be made for the potential for financial markets to improve society. A well-ordered financial system helps individuals and businesses manage risk, and channels savings into productive investments. Robert Shiller, although famous as one of the economists who predicted something like the GFC, has also argued for an expansion of financial markets—for example, to help countries insure each other against the costs of natural disasters (Shiller 2000, 2003, 2013).

But this defence overlooks the fundamental role played by economics in giving birth to modern financial markets. Economists cannot plausibly entirely disinherit the financial monster.

There are other examples of economics shaping the world, although the claim of performativity does not have the same force outside finance. Indeed, there are some areas of economics where we might like it to operate, but it does not. One example is monetary policy, where policy-makers would like their models to convince everyone that inflation will stay on target, but unfortunately they have imperfect credibility. Shiller (2019) nevertheless gives many examples of the way economic theories shape narratives that affect economic outcomes.

This possibility of theory influencing the world, as well as the world influencing the theory, has not been accommodated by the specific kind of economic approach that has been widespread in public policy since the late 1970s. The emphasis has been on markets as the organising principle for the economy and in particular 'free markets'. The role of the state in this view, embedded by the conservative governments of Ronald Reagan and Margaret Thatcher, should be confined to specific 'market failures' or the provision of certain 'public goods'; textbooks give standard examples such as pollution, congestion, or the state provision of basic education. It is important to appreciate that the ideology of a minimal state and expanded 'free markets' only gained such enormous political traction because of the experience by the 1970s of profound 'government failure'

(Coyle 2020b). Like many Britons of my age, I have powerful teen memories of doing homework by candlelight and walking past rubbish piling up on the streets in the late 1970s, as workers in the public sector went on strike. The subsequent privatisation of nationalised industries and deregulation of markets did deliver better services and greater choice. We were finally allowed to take spending money freely on foreign holidays and could get a telephone line without months of waiting.

The economic theories embraced by the Thatcher and Reagan revolution were not the uncontested mainstream at the time, as Keynesian demand management still had many adherents; but the contemporary rational expectations revolution, at its high tide in the early 1980s, was successfully melded to the then-less-fashionable economics of Friedrich von Hayek and economists such as Milton Friedman, who were also part of the Mont Pèlerin group (Stedman Jones 2012; Slobodian 2018). Although academic and professional economists gradually moved away from the abstractions of the rational expectations models, this took some years. This included macroeconomics, which before the GFC remained wedded to overly-simple 'dynamic stochastic general equilibrium' models (Wren-Lewis 2012b). It also, crucially, included the standard 'neoclassical' economics applied to questions of public policy. Adair Turner, then chairman of the Financial Services Authority, highlighted this in a post-crisis speech:

> The neoclassical approach does tend to dictate a particular regulatory philosophy, in which policymakers ideally seek to identify the specific market imperfections preventing the attainment of complete and efficient markets, and in which regulatory intervention should ideally be focussed, not on banning products or dampening down the volatility of

markets, but on disclosure and transparency requirements which will ensure that markets are as efficient as possible.

These propositions, and the strongly free market implications drawn from them, have played a somewhat dominant role in academic economics over the last several decades, though with dissenting voices always present. But they have been even more dominant among policymakers in some of the finance ministries, central banks and regulators of the developed world. Keynes famously suggested that, 'Practical men, who believe themselves quite exempt from any intellectual influences, are normally the slaves of some defunct economist.' But the bigger danger may be that the reasonably intellectual men and women who play key policy-making roles, are often the slaves to a simplified version of the predominant conventional wisdom of the current generation of academic economists (Turner 2010; Keynes 1936).

Academic economics has moved on substantially, but for more than a quarter of a century the scope of markets as a means of organising public as well as private economic activity has expanded. The 1980s privatisation of formerly nationalised industries is just one example. Even though these industries are still regulated by the government, the intellectual framework for this regulation is, as Turner described, the correction of a well-defined 'market failure', a specified reason such as an externality or information asymmetry for a breach in the general principle of the desirability of markets. The boundaries of the economic activities that take place in the public rather than the private sector clearly vary from country to country, suggesting there is room for debate about whether the market can and should organise, say, the supply of water and electricity, or rail and air services, or health care, in part or as a whole.

The share of government spending in the economy has been on an upward trend everywhere over long periods of time, so it is hard to argue that markets are displacing government extensively. However, the market mindset has been applied to the business of government itself, under the rubric of New Public Management. The logic of rational choice was first introduced to politics and administration by James Buchanan and Gordon Tullock in their 1962 book, *The Calculus of Consent: Logical Foundations of Constitutional Democracy*. The introduction of the idea that incentives determine administrative or policy decisions as well as economic choices in the marketplace paved the way for the far wider introduction of the calculus of incentives in public life.

This approach, like the donning of market failure spectacles to circumscribe the government's role in economic management, is still very much alive. Yet there is a backlash against some aspects of it, including the use of quantitative performance targets that clearly divert the behaviour of public sector workers towards the achievement of their specific targets rather than the fulfilment of their underlying purposes. The contracting out of public services to private tender has become increasingly controversial even as it has spread widely. This includes areas once considered properly the domain of government such as the criminal justice system, with the private sector running prisons for profit, or providing sentencing algorithms. Nevertheless, regardless of the controversies, the philosophy of using incentives only, rather than invoking ethos or values or professionalism, to extract a better performance from the public sector is as live as ever in current political debate. So too is the use of competition (or 'contestability') in the delivery of public services.

Unease about the growing scope of markets pre-dates the financial crisis, not least because it has become clear through experience that creating incentives for desired behaviours is a subtler and more difficult matter than the early architects of public service reform imagined. In his bestseller *What Money Can't Buy: The Moral Limits of Markets* (2012), Michael Sandel articulated this forcefully, arguing that economics is to blame for the extension of markets and market-like thinking into wholly inappropriate spheres of life. His view is that markets have led to a degradation of moral and civic values, because they introduce an inappropriate mode of valuation: marketisation of areas such as prisons, policing, and war through the use of commercial providers has corrupted the democratic ideal of citizenship. Sandel writes that we must, 'Call into question an assumption that informs much market-oriented thinking. This is the assumption that all goods are commensurable, that all goods can be translated without loss into a single measure or unit of value' (Sandel 2012, 104). Another philosopher, Elizabeth Anderson, eloquently expressed the same point about the importance of different types of values—while accepting that when public policy decisions are made they either implicitly or explicitly collapse these into a single judgement (Anderson 1993). These reservations about the scope of markets strike a chord with many people.

The crisis gave the critics of economics—or at least what they perceive to be its role in shaping so much of society in the image of markets—plenty of ammunition. The pressure for a formal economists' code of ethics was strong enough to persuade the American Economic Association into drafting one, albeit amounting to a statement of basic integrity for any researcher, the requirement to declare funding sources, in order to be published in an AEA journal.[7] There have been

---

7. The AEA Code of Professional Conduct was adopted on 20 April 2018, https://www.aeaweb.org/about-aea/code-of-conduct. The UK's Royal Economic Society followed in 2019: https://www.res.org.uk/resources-page/code-of-conduct-pdf.html.

other responses in the profession too, among them the growing voice of internal critics. For example, there is an Institute for New Economic Thinking sponsoring conferences and research, and an active Rethinking Economics group. Groups such as these, internationally organised, contest what they see as the monolithic nature of mainstream economics. They have a point; several Nobel prize winners have argued that the 'Top Five' economics journals are too narrow a funnel for professional academic success (Akerlof 2020; Heckman and Moktan 2020). Mainstream economists tend to be too dismissive of the critics, either the non-economists who (wrongly) believe economics is only about marketisation or the economists who identify themselves as 'heterodox' as against an overly-narrow mainstream. There is plenty of empirical research suggesting that in many contexts, including public service provision, market structures do lead to more desirable outcomes than direct government management. However, economists know—as non-economists often do not—that the character of what you might call mainstream economics itself has changed substantially during the past twenty-five years (Coyle 2010). In many areas of economics the free market version that shaped so much public policy from the late 1970s is long gone, replaced by a more capacious modern mainstream that combines the conventional emphasis on the power of incentives and the inevitability of choice with a more recent evidence-driven understanding of human psychology, the effects of technology, the importance of institutions and culture, and the long shadow of history.

For example, economists have been eager adopters of so-called behavioural models and findings from cognitive science that demonstrate that the standard rational choice assumptions of conventional economics are invalid in some circumstances. There is an active field of research (one I have reservations about) that is exploring the contexts in which new behavioural assumptions need to be applied, and how, and the implications of doing so for economic policy. Similarly, institutional economics sees collective decisions as being more than the sum of separate individual decisions. It recognises that people have different interests and that politics (with either a small or a large 'p'), history, and culture will have an important effect on economics. Economic history and sociology generally are exerting greater influence on mainstream economics. Research is alive to issues such as asymmetries of information and transactions costs affecting economic choices.

This means that much of the framework that academic economists now habitually use bears little relation to the everyday economics debated in politics and applied in public policy. Paradoxically, commentators who are very critical of 'economics' often celebrate leading economists practising in this eclectic modern mainstream. The idea of economics co-opted into policy-making in such an enduring way by Mr Reagan and Mrs Thatcher has been retained for too long outside the profession. Many of us have long known that economics as it is actually practised has become much subtler than the public version, but perhaps too few have said so, prolonging the misperception that we are all free market ideologues. Perhaps we need to communicate better the breadth of 'mainstream' research, while acknowledging at the same time that it has shortcomings such as the Top Five journal bottleneck.

Part of the explanation for a reluctance to communicate may be a kind of professional courtesy to one branch of economics, albeit an important one. That is macroeconomics, a specialism of relatively few professional economists, but absolutely dominant in the public eye. Normal people think that macroeconomics, forecasting economy-wide outcomes such as inflation and growth, interest rates or the level of government borrowing, is what all economists do. Macroeconomic forecasting is certainly an important function, and is covered by the media constantly (see Chapter Two for more on macroeconomics). Most economists never produce a forecast, but rather work on a very wide variety of subjects from innovation to health care to pensions. In the UK at least, the outcome of the 2016 Brexit vote swung most of the economics profession decisively into the camp of needing to communicate far more often and far better with the public. Nine out of ten professional economists considered that leaving the EU would lead to worse UK economic performance, and indeed many said so publicly during the campaign;[8] the message, obviously, did not resonate with just over half of the people who voted.

MARKETS AS A PROCESS

Economics has long had internal dissenters, who felt wholly vindicated by the GFC, and believe the moment has come for a 'paradigm shift' in economics (Kuhn 1996 [1962]). My argument is that the mainstream of economics was never monolithic, and anyway has been changing gradually but significantly for over more than two decades. Its centre of gravity has moved away from theory to applied work, away from macroeconomics to microeconomics, and away from theoretical abstraction to institutional and behavioural detail. This shift does not mean that the majority professional opinion has abandoned markets, however. Most economists consider markets as generally a

8. Sonia Sodha, Toby Helm, and Phillip Inman, 'Economists Overwhelmingly Reject Brexit in Boost for Cameron', *The Guardian*, 28 May 2016, https://www.theguardian.com/politics/2016/may/28/economists-reject-brexit-boost-cameron.

better way where possible than direct government intervention of organising the economy, still often advocate market solutions (such as carbon trading or school vouchers) for policy problems, remain convinced about the broad merits of trade liberalisation, and so on. Such instincts are generally justified by evidence based on specific applied research. If the evidence suggests an active government role, economists will recommend it; and indeed in the decade since the GFC there has been a widespread shift in sentiment in this direction. Whatever you think about the approach, the idea of the 'nudge', whereby policies recognise psychological realities such as inertia or the effect of how people's choices are 'framed', is one example of a new interventionism. Market design is a vibrant area of economics combining market processes with the deliberate shaping of the rules by which they operate, used in policy areas such as auctions of government bonds or radio spectrum. The experience of the Covid19 pandemic has made massive government economic intervention a reality anyway.

What is the basis of our economists' underlying instinct to trust markets? The broad idea of 'general equilibrium' is an important principle, making the point that everything in the economy is connected and the full consequences of any action can be far reaching. It is a useful inoculation against the temptation to indulge in social engineering, because it is so hard to think through all the possible consequences of any action or policy. General equilibrium as a specific theory is an abstract, ideal world of identical individuals making their own choices according to pre-determined preferences, with no transactions costs or externalities. With these assumptions, it is possible to prove that competitive equilibrium will replicate the decisions of an omniscient and benign central planner. In these abstract conditions, the market—a series of trades between individuals regulated by price—is the most efficient way of discovering and satisfying individual preferences. This approach, with its implication that markets are the benchmark best way to organise the economy, is taught to graduate students of economics. It is highly mathematical, and I for one barely scraped through this course. Only those few economists who go on to become pure theorists and teach general equilibrium theory to their successor cohorts need to think deeply about the specifics again. But economists' market-oriented instincts (luckily) do not depend on understanding mathematical fixed-point theorems. For markets are far more useful in practice than they are in theory. Market economies have made many people better off, innovating in ways that improve our lives, enabling us to make the choices that best suit us, given the constraints of income and time.

It is important to distinguish between markets as a source and description of value, which is what critics like Michael Sandel challenge, and markets as a process for orchestrating economic activity. These are often confused, including by many economists who strongly prefer using a market price as either the best or the only means of assigning value. However, Sandel is surely correct to argue that some values cannot be meaningfully expressed in terms of money, and that to do so can seem to demean other important (non-monetary) values. We economists would do better to accept that many people find it genuinely unethical to put a price on biodiversity or the climate, even as we argue that price mechanisms—market processes—can help protect species or reduce CO_2 emissions. It would make for a more fruitful conversation with our critics.

What markets do brilliantly, nevertheless, is co-ordinate the use of resources in a process of discovery and challenge. The information signalled by the price set by demand and supply is a wonderful co-ordinating device. Many economists have described this co-ordination eloquently. Here is Paul Seabright:

> This morning I went out and bought a shirt. . . . The shirt I bought, although a simple item by the miracle of modern technology, represents a triumph of international coordination. The cotton was grown in India, from seeds developed in the United States; the artificial fibre in the thread comes from Portugal and the material in the dyes from at least six other countries; the collar linings come from Brazil, and the machinery for weaving, cutting and sewing from Germany; the shirt itself was made up in Malaysia. The project of making a shirt and delivering it to me in Toulouse has been a long time in the planning, since well before the morning two winters ago when an Indian farmer led a pair of ploughing bullocks across his land on the red plains outside Coimbatore. Engineers in Cologne and chemists in Birmingham were involved in the preparation many years ago. . . . And yet I am sure that nobody knew I was going to be buying a shirt of this kind today (Seabright 2010).

We accept of course that in many cases the market price excludes important information, such as the true cost of CO_2 emissions from the burning of fossil fuels, or the negative (loss of privacy) and positive (useful aggregated information) from sharing data with a tech company. Nevertheless, the catastrophic economic (never mind political) failure of the communist planned economies by 1989 demonstrated the inability in practice of a central planner to replicate this information-coordinating process. Even with today's far more powerful computers, 'big' data and AI, there are good reasons to believe planning would fail, as Chapter Six will discuss.

Competitive markets also provide an unrivalled way of changing the allocation of resources over time. John Kay has described this function as a 'discovery process'. Joseph Schumpeter (1994 [1942]) famously referred to it as 'creative destruction'. The competitive process is the source of dynamism in the economy—innovation, the invention and production of new goods and services, growth. Other types of economic organisation, including central planners, can sustain growth for a period, perhaps quite a long period (see Acemoglu and Robinson 2012). But most new goods and services, the source of the astonishing increase in prosperity for the past quarter of a millennium, would not have become available without market capitalism.

It is important to underline the word 'competitive' in this statement. There is confusion between markets and business in public debate. As Adam Smith famously pointed out in *The Wealth of Nations*, businessmen will naturally be inclined to combine against the public interest to improve their profits. A 'pro-business' policy helping a large company or an oligopolistic sector of the economy make more money is not at all the same as a 'pro-market' or 'pro-economy' policy, although the distinction is often elided. Economists love competition, while businesses hate it; as Andy Grove of Intel famously put it in the title of his 1988 book, competition means 'only the paranoid survive' in business. The benefits of markets depend on the existence of competition between suppliers, whereas businesses prefer its absence. And, yes, some economists do take the corporate shilling and make pro-business rather than pro-market, pro-competition arguments.

Competition is quite a tender plant. Politicians and regulators need to be vigilant against incumbents' interest in keeping out new entrants and inhibiting competition. The more successful, the larger, the more profitable and powerful the incumbents, the harder it is to maintain competition. Every so often in democracies, the accretion of corporate interest is swept away on a tide of popular indignation. The classic instance is the trust-busting and breakup of giants such as Standard Oil in the United States in the 1910s, thanks to the investigations of journalist Ida Tarbell. The period of legal activism against big business was succeeded by populism and anger as the 1929 stock market crash and economic downturn collided with high levels of inequality and Jazz Age conspicuous consumption. The present context is disturbingly similar. A number of recent reports have concluded that the digital sector, dominated by a handful of titanic US companies, needs shaking up to enhance competition (Crémer, Montjoye, and Schweitzer 2019; Furman et al. 2019; Scott-Morton et al. 2019). There is certainly now a similar imperative to ensure that markets are competitive, and are not rigged in favour of incumbent corporate interests. We cannot be at all confident this is the case now, in the United States and many European economies (Philippon 2019; Bajgar et al. 2019).

The role of markets as a discovery process is fundamental. The reason was set out by Hayek in a classic article, 'The Use of Knowledge in Society', namely that markets co-ordinate information about what he describes as 'unorganized' knowledge, "the knowledge of the particular circumstances of time and place" (Hayek 1945, 521). This detail can never, by its nature, be aggregated or turned into statistics. It can only be used in a decentralized way. He writes: 'The most significant fact about this system is the economy of knowledge with which it operates, or how little the individual participants need to know in order to be able to take the right action. In abbreviated form, by a kind of symbol, only the most essential information is passed on and passed on only to those concerned' (Hayek 1945, 526–527).

The advantages of markets as a co-ordination and discovery process do not over-ride the disadvantages of markets as a means of valuation in some circumstances, however. Because, of course, the two functions co-exist. To allocate economic resources of one kind or another through a market is at the same time usually to put a monetary price on them. Economists have not often enough acknowledged the force of what we could call the Sandel critique. There are circumstances in which a less efficient mechanism for allocation should be preferable because non-monetary values outweigh monetary ones. His examples centre on the value of civic participation, the 'republican virtues'. Others come from the domain of fairness. Rationing in wartime invariably gives rise to so-called black markets, which the authorities have to spend much effort stamping out. The conventional (or perhaps caricature in this context) economic view would be that price is the most efficient rationing device: if supply is restricted, the best use of scarce resources is to allocate them to people who value them the most as reflected in their willingness to pay a higher price. Similar arguments are made about rent controls or controls on foreign exchange. But access to food or clothes in wartime is not the same as access to the housing market in normal times. Similar arguments explain why regulators acted against price gouging during the 2020 lockdowns, stamping out or punishing big hikes in prices of medical supplies and essentials. All citizens must be in the same boat, even if the result is some allocative inefficiency, when there is a national emergency such as war or pandemic. The non-monetary value of fairness trumps price signals and market efficiency.

However, we ought to be clear—and clearer than Sandel is—about when civic values outweigh market values, and when market processes are useful even if we want to apply a non-monetary mode of valuing outcomes. Many people would agree with his examples concerning warfare, or justice: we do not want a market in evading the draft or in buying the desired outcome of a trial. He argues for excluding medicine from the market—should only the rich be able to buy a kidney or heart? Most Britons, devoted to the more or less free-to-use National Health Service (NHS), agree. Here, though, the difference between values and processes is relevant. Economics Nobel Prize winner Al Roth—someone who has given much thought to what he describes as 'repugnant' markets—designed a kidney exchange; no money changes hands, yet it is organised as a market matching suppliers and users. Within just a few years of his innovation, thirty people in New England had received kidneys—without putting a price on them—through this market (Roth, Sönmez, and Ünver 2004; Roth 2007).[9] By now, thousands of people around the world have benefited.

Keeping conceptually separate markets as processes for matching supply and demand, and markets as a way of putting a price on everything might help evaluate the kinds of circumstances in which we would want to apply a civic or intrinsic values over-ride. This distinction, for example, is at the heart of periodic UK debate about the organisation of the NHS. Proponents of reform insist that they do not intend to challenge the general principle of tax-funded free health care at the point of use, and get irritated that opponents are equally insistent that the hidden aim is privatisation. Both sides misunderstand each other to some extent. Some opponents of proposals for

9. Kidney exchanges have now been widely used in a number of countries, https://www.bbc.co.uk/news/business-50632630. The UK Living Kidney Sharing Scheme carried out its 1,000th transplant in March 2019.

extending the domain of markets in UK health care object on grounds of fairness—preferring rationing by waiting list to rationing by price—and on grounds of civic participation— the NHS being one of the most important civic institutions in this country, binding us together through common experi- ence. This was highlighted in 2012 when it featured prominently in the opening ceremony of the London Olympic Games, a celebration of the best of British. The 2020 experience of the Covid19 pandemic, when Britons applauded the NHS from their doorsteps weekly during lockdown, sent the same mes- sage. Although some are ideologues, at least some supporters of reform seek to introduce the discovery process of competi- tive supply to improve NHS efficiency and do not see this as amounting to privatisation or making monetary values para- mount. It might be helpful to the political debate to be more explicit about the distinctions.

THE BEHAVIOURAL FIX

So far this chapter has been arguing that economics does bear some responsibility for shaping reality in its theoretical image—to an important degree in financial markets and to a lesser degree in marketising society—although political ide- ology and the wider intellectual framework of public policy have also played a significant part. The policy environment has over-relied on the free market, rational expectations models of neoclassical economics for considerably longer than have many academic economists.

I have nevertheless strongly supported economists' advo- cacy of market competition as an essential process for the efficient allocation of resources. Competing against other pro- ducers encourages the efficient use of resources at any point in time and the innovation of new products and services over time. When we talk about economic growth, what we really mean is innovation, new ideas that improve people's lives. GDP growth is not just more bread or more clothes; it is also new medicines, a wider range of book titles, undreamt-of artefacts like the internet and smartphones, the opportunity to travel to other countries, and visit the cinema or attend the Olympics (Coyle 2014). Human curiosity alone would have brought many discoveries, but commercial imperatives and the pressure of contesting for customers in markets are needed to translate discovery into services and products that are produced at scale, are affordable, and improve many people's lives. It is new ideas, made mass reality, that have enriched us over the centuries.

Yet economists should also acknowledge that markets have limitations as a measure of value. As well as the classic list of market failures such as pollution or needing to pay for defence, not all values are measured in terms of prices. Non-monetary values should and will trump monetary measures in certain contexts. It is not always easy to spell out what is the proper domain of profits and prices, and where instead other values such as fairness or civic engagement over-ride markets. The boundary varies from country to country, has shifted over time, and continues to be a matter of political debate. Even so, the critique of the emphasis on markets in economics can be addressed by the distinction between their functions as a process for organising activity and as a measure of value.

However, there is another objection critics of economics often make, namely that it is obviously false to assume that people are rational and selfish, and therefore economics, in making that assumption, must be fundamentally in error. How can we model people's economic behaviour without the foundational assumption of rational self-interest?

Economists have responded with an intense interest in behavioural psychology. If there are non-rational 'biases' in human behaviour that we can incorporate as variations into our analysis, most economists cheerfully do so. By these I mean predictable ways in which people diverge from the broadly self-interested calculating logic based on all available information and fixed preferences, as assumed by conventional economic models. There is quite a long list of such biases, including framing effects (how choices are described), endowment effects (we value more what we already have), over-optimism compared to objective probabilities, and so on. Daniel Kahneman (2011) explains these as the result of the interplay between 'fast' and 'slow' thinking, which occur in different parts of the brain. Fast thinking comprises rules of thumb and intuitive choices, and is the norm. Slow thinking is the rational calculation, which is hard work given our brain structure and therefore costly in terms of energy. Conventional economics has been based on the assumption of slow thinking, but is slowly incorporating fast thinking as well, in the form of behavioural rules of thumb.

This methodological fix has its limits. One is that it is not wholly clear when to apply either the rational or the behavioural assumptions. Kahneman shared the Economics Nobel memorial prize in 2002 with Vernon Smith, whose experimental work has shown that people's spur of the moment 'fast' decisions often lead to exactly the outcomes that conventional rationality-based economics would predict. Other researchers looking at animal behaviour have shown that pigeons, rats, bees and capuchin monkeys in trading for food also act like rational, calculating *homo economicus*. As Keith Stanovich (2005) put it, 'The behavior of many non-human animals does in fact follow pretty closely the axioms of rational choice.' Self-interest and competition drive evolutionary success. Within the brain, each individual neuron acts like *homo economicus*. What comes to our conscious attention is the result of a ferocious competition between perceptually-triggered neurons to rise through successive layers of the brain, subject to an energy constraint. The descriptions of cognitive scientists suggest this process could be successfully modelled as a classic constrained-optimisation problem borrowed from economics (IDEI 2011). So it seems that people undertake 'slow' thinking in some contexts. This might just be a matter of simplicity: as Stanovich points out, either simple minds (as in a pigeon) or a simple environment makes rational choice all the easier. Robert Aumann (2008), Gerd Gigerenzer (2007), and others suggest that we adopt rules of thumb, fast thinking rules, that usually result in rationally optimal decisions, but sometimes not. One could describe it as rational non-rationality.

Chapter Three will return to other problems raised by the use of behavioural economics in policy choices, concerning the presumption that government interventions can lead people to better choices—whose definition of 'better' is this? Here I want to note that this is the latest in a number of examples of borrowing between economics and other human sciences. Malthus' essay on population inspired Darwin (Browne 2003). He in his turn inspired social scientists ranging from the distortions of social Darwinists to Karl Marx (whose request to dedicate *Das Kapital* to him Darwin politely declined). Evolution has ever since been used, at least as a metaphor, by any economist who studies business and markets, as competition is indeed a kind of survival of the fittest. Game theory offers another example of fruitful exchange between biology and economics. John Maynard Smith (1976), with George Price (1973), borrowed the concept for evolutionary game theory, and the subsequent work of biologists fed back into economists' thinking about altruism and reciprocity. The intellectual exchange continued with the application to the economy, especially the financial sector, of the models of complexity and networks used in ecology (for example, Haldane and May 2011).

This lengthy mutual inspiration between economics and biology is easy to understand. Economics is fundamentally a part of natural science as well as a part of the humanities. One of the founding fathers of economics, David Hume, saw his political economy as part of the same intellectual project as understanding refraction or reasoning about how we can get from perception to knowledge. Its ambition is to discover how individual and social choices about the use of resources, shaped as they are by history and culture, fit into the natural universe. Modern economics must stay true to all these intellectual roots. C. P. Snow, remembered for dividing knowledge into 'two cultures' in fact concluded, in later reflecting on the discussion about his famous lecture (Snow 1963 [1959]), that there are three. He populated this third culture with the social sciences:

I have been increasingly impressed by a body of intellectual opinion, forming itself, without organisation, without any kind of lead or conscious direction, under the surface of this debate. This body of opinion seems to come from intellectual persons in a variety of fields—social history, sociology, demography, political science, economics, government (in the American academic sense), psychology, medicine, and social arts such as architecture. It seems a mixed bag, but there is an inner consistency. All of them are concerned with how human beings are living or have lived—and concerned, not in terms of legend, but in fact (quoted in Gould 2003, 42).

Critics of economics do not like its ambition to be part of empirical, natural science. The subject has often been accused of physics envy, as if this were a terrible crime. The accusation often boils down to a charge of being too mechanistic, or too reductionist, which is a different matter. The accusers do not seem to mind as much economists being inspired by biology (or for that matter by a different kind of technique from physics such as the non-linear dynamics of phase transitions). It might be objected that economics cannot be located in the sciences because its methodology can never be experimental, like the natural sciences. Even an event like the crisis of 2008 or 2020 does not provide experimental evidence because it is contingent; today's circumstances are too different, even from those of the 1920s and 1930s, to enable generalisation. However, not only are experimental methods and randomised control trials increasingly being used in economics, the natural sciences themselves do not offer as many pure demonstrations of the classic, experimental scientific method as one might think. As Stephen Jay Gould put it:

A large range of factual subjects, evidently part of science and duly explainable (in principle) by empirical methods operating under natural laws, treats different kinds of inordinately complex and historically contingent systems—the history of continents and landforms, or the pattern of life's phylogeny, for example—as not deducible, or predictable at all, from natural laws tested and applied in laboratory experiments, but crucially dependent on the unique character of antecedent historical states in a narrative sequence fully subject to explanation after the fact, but unpredictable beforehand (Gould 2003, 42).

He argued that natural scientists underplay narrative, historical explanations, thereby restricting their official toolkit unnecessarily. The same argument could apply to economics.

Economics sits alongside evolutionary theory and cognitive science as well as alongside sociology and political science. But it is a difficult subject because—as this chapter began—it can change the reality it is studying. Imagine if Dr Frankenstein had intended not only to create life but also to anticipate in advance everything the creature might do when it gained consciousness, and then to adjust his creation to take account of that otherwise changed world, thus averting its rampage. Or to use a different image, economics is like meteorology, a vast, complex non-linear dynamic system but with atmospheric variables that are conscious and self-conscious. This generates the self-fulfilling and self-averting properties described earlier: if an economist could accurately predict a financial crash or recession—and policy-makers and others acted on the prediction—would it either cause or prevent this from happening?

Economists certainly need to be modest about how little progress we have made; but we must resist regarding the subject as anything less than a part of the great intellectual voyage of modern science. The GFC helped both on the modesty front and with the substance of sending some economists back to questions of what we can actually know, rather than what we theorise. It is difficult to make a public admission of error, and all the more so for academics who are professionally identified with certain ideas and theories. Some of them are offering spirited resistance to criticism. However, the shock is welcome if it re-roots economics in detailed observation of people's and businesses' behaviour, as well as downloading big data sets and applying statistical techniques to them.

RESPONSIBLE ECONOMICS

Rather than Keynes's 'humble, competent' dentists, or Duflo's plumbers, economists perhaps need to be more like laboratory technicians—not Dr Frankenstein but his cautious assistant. For several reasons, the recent past has seen a vast amount of careful, detailed empirical work in economics. Computers mean many more data sets have been created, accessed, and shared. Statistical techniques for analysing economic data have improved, and techniques such as experiments and randomized control trials have become more widely used. There is always a need for greater care, but the interaction of theory and evidence is central to advancing understanding.

It is an irony that all this work, flooding out daily in working papers, and including interaction with other disciplines such as psychology, epidemiology, engineering, and history, is being undertaken without much changing the public image of economics as being so dismal. This suggests that economists have yet to succeed in one important lesson from recent experience. That is the need for a science that can alter the world to engage with the world, to participate in debate and promote public conversation about what economists do now. Greater engagement has started. For example, economists are prominent in the blogosphere, more so than other social and natural scientists (Thoma 2011). Similarly, many engage in debate on social media. This is all to the good, because economists do have specific public responsibilities and need to be held accountable.

Part II: Why Is Economics Special?

Why is there no Government Chief Anthropologist? Many countries appoint natural scientists and economists, but usually not other social scientists, to prominent official roles. Why do economists have so central a role in policy-making, and is that status justified? This chapter has so far discussed the influence of the subject of economics on the world—in a specific way in financial markets and also in the broad sense of shaping the intellectual, and consequently the practical, framework within which political and policy debates take place. What about the direct influence of economists on policy-making—both the ample commentary by academic and think tank economists on specific policies, and the important role of economists in government? What are the responsibilities this influence entails?

My professional life as an economist began with a couple of years in the British Treasury. A few thousands of economists altogether work in the UK in government: in Whitehall departments, in regulatory agencies, in the Bank of England and financial regulators, and in local government and its satellite bodies. Figure 1 shows how the number in central government has grown (it had reached around 2000 by 2020, thanks to a big recruitment drive for Brexit preparation).

The specific tasks vary greatly, but one survey of Government Economic Service (GES) members asked them to categorise their work. Overwhelmingly they described their main task as communicating the results of technical economic analysis to non-specialists, either their non-economist colleagues or politicians (see Portes 2012).[10] Communication, influencing the public debate, is also one of the main functions of the many hundreds of other economists who circle the public policy world in think

10. See also Jonathan Portes, 'Economists in Government: What Are They Good For?' http://notthetreasuryview.blogspot.co.uk/2012/01/economists-in-government-what-are-they.html, 12 January 2012, accessed 30 April 2012, Survey for GES by Paul Anand, Open University, and Jonathan Leape, London School of Economics.

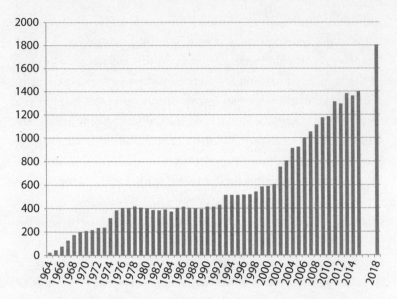

FIGURE 1. Number of members of UK Government Economic Service. Source: GES

tanks or as academics urged by their funding bodies to develop and demonstrate the policy impact of their research. Policy economics, this strongly suggests, is an activity of persuasion.

I suggested earlier that there is a lag between the kind of economics generally practised in the academic world today and the economics being implemented in the policy world. While mainstream economic research has moved progressively beyond the reductive rational expectations, free market versions of the 1980s, official policy economics has probably changed less. This sort of lag is inevitable. Keynes, endlessly quotable, warned about the enduring influence of economic ideas that are past their use-by date: 'Madmen in authority, who hear voices in the air, are distilling their frenzy from some academic scribbler of a few years back' (Keynes 1936). This is perhaps an overly-dramatic way of making the point that one can hardly expect people outside the academic world to stay on top of frontier research as well as doing their day job.

However, here I want to make two other points. One is that there is a core paradox in policy economics: economic analysis in the world of policy almost always takes the perspective of an objective, omniscient outsider whose benign aim is to maximise social welfare; but by putting economics into practice through public policy, the policy economist cannot avoid stepping into the model. The economist is not able to act as a deus ex machina. Policies have to be implemented by policy-makers, including economists, and the implementation of policy is so fraught with difficulty that there is a well-known phenomenon of 'government failure' alongside 'market failure'. Much has been written about the endless examples of policies that not only do not work—such as costly IT systems that get scrapped or big projects which cost billions more than planned—but even backfire. One example will stand for thousands: the US 'cash for clunkers' scheme in 2009 was intended to boost the revenues of the struggling auto industry. When people turned in their old car, they received a payment to put towards a cleaner new car—meant to help the environment at the same time as GM. The scheme in fact reduced the industry's revenues. The policy analysts had not taken into account that in cash-strapped times people would use the subsidy to downgrade to smaller, albeit more fuel-efficient, cars (Hoekstra, Puller, and West 2017).

Yet economic policy analyses pay remarkably little attention to questions of implementation, including behavioural response. Government failure risks should be as much part of policy analysis as market failures.

The second point concerns the broader interaction between economics and politics. At one level, pressures spilling over from political imperatives mean that economists often end up appearing or claiming to be certain where they are deeply uncertain, while at the same time being too diffident about expressing inconvenient truths about which we can be much more certain. At a deeper level, there is a tension between the technical expertise of economics and democratic legitimacy, a tension that became more evident after the GFC in Greece and Italy, and subsequently in many other countries including Brexit Britain. Populism and technocracy sit uneasily together. It is high time economists gave careful thought to the political economy of policy economics.

It is worth emphasising to start with that the discipline of economics is fundamental for good policy-making. Its benefits are not always visible, but they are pervasive. It is important to set out first just why economics should have its special role in public policy.

One absolutely fundamental concept the subject brings to decision making in government is opportunity cost. This is really just a statement about physics, that time runs forward and that resources used in one activity are not available for an alternative. Economics is the study of choice between alternatives. Opportunity cost is unpopular in the world of politics, however. Politicians reflect their voters' preference for having your cake *and* eating it. Politicians therefore might not like economists—but they need them.

Another fundamental idea is cost-benefit analysis (CBA). In the UK there is an elaborate set of rules for doing this, set out in a how-to manual known as the Green Book.[11] In the United States, Ronald Reagan introduced a requirement for a cost-benefit

11. The approach is set out in the Treasury's Green Book documentation, http://www.hm-treasury.gov.uk/data_greenbook_index.htm.

analysis for many new regulations—although President Trump was less keen on using such evidence (Shapiro 2020). CBA consists of trying to list and measure where possible all the likely results of a policy. Those that can be measured are converted into monetary terms, and the costs and benefits netted off against each other. This analysis can lend an assumption-laden exercise a spurious precision, which is recognised in the guidance although generally ignored in practice. It certainly over-privileges effects that can be directly measured and monetized. Many economists (including me [Coyle and Sensier 2020], but also Hausman [2012]) have been critical of the way cost-benefit analysis is implemented. But it is always better to make decisions aware that there are costs and benefits, and with some systematic framework for assessing them. When they are not made explicit, there will always be an implicit judgement, just as there is when we make choices in everyday life.

Ronald Coase (1960) also pointed out that a cost-benefit analysis of any policy also needs to put the costs of the policy action itself into the judgement. The government economist is part of the equation she is assessing:

> It is clear that the government has powers which might enable it to get some things done at a lower cost than could a private organisation. . . . But the governmental administrative machine is not itself costless. It can in fact on occasion be extremely costly. Furthermore there is no reason to suppose that the restrictive . . . regulations, made by a fallible administration subject to political pressures and operating without any competitive check, will necessarily always be those which increase the efficiency with which the economic system operates.

As he continues, 'All solutions have costs.' A specific policy or regulation may solve one problem but cause others elsewhere, and those effects need to be incorporated into the assessment. Coase attributed the many examples of government failure to economists' habit of seeing their job as fixing a problem in a particular context without considering the way behaviour will change as a result. He also described a 'looseness of thought' stemming from failing to compare a particular course of action to a clear alternative—often the status quo or do nothing option.

My experience of Whitehall decisions, first as a government economist myself, and later as a member of various policy committees and regulatory bodies, is that they are well-intentioned but too often flawed for these reasons. Even so, a systematic framework for setting out the pros and cons of a decision, and making clear what is evidenced and what is a matter of judgement, is an essential discipline.[12]

Those two related concepts between them, the opportunity cost of a course of action and the need to weigh its costs and benefits in a systematic way, are alone enough to justify the privileged role of economics in government. They impose a discipline on policy choices that would otherwise be absent. However, the distinctive contribution of economics in policy analysis goes beyond these basics. What's more, this contribution has been improving, thanks to the increasing availability of data, more computer power, and sophisticated statistical methods for analysing data. Applied microeconomics can bring

12. The concept of public value provides an alternative and more explicitly judgemental approach. It is essentially a cost-benefit analysis that recognises the inherent difficulty of comparing incommensurate or even unmeasurable variables (Coyle and Woolard 2009).

a powerful lens to decisions across a wide range of areas of economic and social policy.

Examples abound in applied economic analysis of the way markets operate. Transport economics has had many policy applications. Daniel McFadden was co-recipient of the 2000 Nobel memorial prize for his development of econometric methods for predicting passenger demand, as applied in a now-classic example to San Francisco's BART authority (McFadden 1974). Economists have developed road pricing mechanisms and congestion charges. In many places, before the days of ride-sharing services, there were shortages of taxis, sustained by barriers to entry in the form of licences. A taxi licence or medallion was a valuable piece of property, and incumbents ardently resisted the issue of new ones no matter how acute the taxi shortage. This made the regulation of fares essential: otherwise taxi owners and drivers could extract large mono-poly rents from their customers. One neat proposal based on economic analysis was a 1997 proposal to improve the Dublin taxi market by issuing a second licence to all existing hold-ers, who could then sell them on. The incumbents were thus compensated at least in the short term for the dilution of their original property rights (Fingleton, Evans, and Hogan 1998).

Other arenas of policy where market analysis is fundamen-tal include industry regulation and competition policy. Econo-mists working in these areas have more reason than most to know that the assumptions of competitive 'free' markets and rational choice are unlikely to be valid. They draw on a long-standing tradition of analysing departures from competition, as well as increasingly on the newer behavioural economics literature as applied to consumer choice. One nice example of why competition authorities are paying more attention to behavioural economics is given by Rufus Pollock, who looked at why deregulation of directory inquiries in the UK in 2003 failed to improve competition in that market. He concluded that consumers, faced with a wide range of unfamiliar numbers combined with limitations on their capacity to process information, gravitated toward one (The Number) that was easy to remember, 118 118, and was marketed with genius, the advertising campaign using identical twins. The companies that bought seemingly more advantageous numbers made the same mistake as the regulators in their assumptions about consumer behaviour—for instance, that numbers ending in 000 would be more memorable (Pollock 2009). There was a rather dramatic concentration of this supposedly more competitive market. Standard consumer theory did not serve well here.

Results like this mean that economists working in public policy or bodies like competition or industry regulators are now hungry to make better use of behavioural economics in their work.

There are very many more examples. Clever economics in designing and implementing an auction of 3G spectrum rights to telecommunications companies netted the UK government £22.5bn in a 2000 auction, about 2.5 percent of GDP at the time (Binmore and Klemperer 2002). The US Federal Communications Commission has been running spectrum auctions since the mid-1990s, raising tens of billions of dollars. Across areas of social and economic policy such as education, health care, welfare benefits, housing, pensions, applied economic analysis is the everyday bread and butter of public policy, in Whitehall, Washington, Brussels, and other capitals, in industry regulators, in some think tanks, and in the academic world. Its techniques are continually improving, thanks in part to the availability of new data sets, or methodological innovations such as Randomised Control Trials (first used in economics in the context of evaluating aid programmes in developing countries and now increasingly for domestic policies in western countries), or better econometric methods. The economics that comes to wider attention, including economic growth forecasts and government budget questions, thus forms the tiny tip of a huge and growing iceberg of policy-relevant applied economics. This work is expanding the potential for improving public policies, rooting policy in solid empirical evidence about its likely effectiveness.

Yet its expansion will be controversial. When evidence and prior belief conflict, it is not at all clear that evidence will win. This is partly politics. As Keynes (yes, again) once said, 'There is nothing a government hates more than to be well-informed; for it makes the process of arriving at decisions much more complicated and difficult' (quoted in Skidelsky 1992, 629). It is also partly about the character of social science, and the possibility of claims to objectivity when the subject of study is—ourselves.

PUTTING ECONOMISTS INTO ECONOMICS

The intellectual machinery of empirical, statistical study of causal relationships in society is distinctive about economics. Other social sciences could not substitute for this in policy-making (although the other social sciences should supplement it, and could certainly do more quantitative empirical research themselves, just as economists could adopt more of their qualitative methods). Economists nevertheless need to take note of a paradox in applying the lessons of social science to society, one whose acuteness increases with the force of the claims being made for the validity of that science. The ideas of economists about the economy can shape the world, as well as merely describing it. Thanks to its role in the political process and policy analysis, economic advice also shapes the world very directly and institutionally. This can often have good outcomes, but the policy economist generally takes the perspective of an objective outsider, benign, rational, even omniscient; and too rarely considers what this perspective implies when economists are (or ought to be) part of what they are modelling. As Coase put it, we need to put ourselves in the scales we are holding in order to weigh the costs against the benefits of any policy intervention. Given the spread of institutions run by economists and embedding economic analysis in how they operate, such as central banks and industry regulators, this is a non-trivial point. It is why some commentators have begun to push back against the 1990s and 2000s trend toward making bodies like central banks and competition authorities independent; for instance, Tucker (2019) argues that they need to acknowledge they are not making technical but rather political or values-based choices.

Economists generally take it for granted that our models are useful tools. We simultaneously assume that they are 'true' in the sense of not being systematically at odds with important features of the real world, and yet not true at all as a faithful description of reality. A parallel often used is the classic diagram of the London Underground, which is a superb guide to travel on the Tube and yet a hopeless representation of the geography of London. As John Sutton has pointed out, our training quickly socializes us to think that this habit of abstraction in order to focus on key features is normal, and we do not really understand critics who believe society is too complicated and messy for this analytical approach to be useful (Sutton 2000). Equally, critics of economics fail to understand that economists do not fundamentally mistake models for the real world, but rather use them as thought experiments to structure the complexity of what we are trying to analyse. However, in using these tools, we economists do habitually take the perspective of the benign divinity, able to see what is happening down below without being seen by the humans (and thus affecting their behaviour). It is a perspective that can reshape behaviour and hence the economic reality in sometimes damaging ways. A key failure in analysing a policy intervention is overlooking the possible behavioural response, a response that changes what needs to be analysed. Small-scale examples are risk compensation (whereby making one thing safer by regulation leads to greater risk-taking in some other aspect so that the overall degree of individual risk in unchanged [Hedlund 2000]) or the unanticipated effect of incentives, as in the 'cash for clunkers' example. Even 'behavioural' policies that are supposed to take account of human psychology are prone to this error of assuming the context is fixed: do traffic 'nudges' make roads safer? It is not known whether, after an initial period when the intervention is novel, people's behaviour reverts to normal. On a large scale, the top-down view from outside the model can lead to adverse consequences: James Scott (1998)—who labels this perspective 'high modernism'—gives many examples of rationalising policies that backfire terribly, such as urban planning restrictions that leach the economic vibrancy out of cities or agricultural subsidies incentivising actions that harm biodiversity and ultimately crop yields.

This self-referential character of policy advice is all the more important given the important institutional role of economics in government. The importance of institutions for the success of an economy has come to prominence in academic research in recent years. In 2009, Elinor Ostrom and Oliver Williamson were jointly awarded the Nobel memorial prize for their work on the economics of institutions. Recently in development economics there has been great emphasis on the need for sound political institutions, including the rule of law but also inclusive institutions enabling successful entrepreneurship and new entry to the economic elite (Besley and Persson 2012; Acemoglu and Robinson 2012). The more recent institutional economics is also descended from the public choice school, which emphasises the role of incentives in politics and government as well as in purely 'economic' decisions. Mancur Olson argued that a successful economy depends on government overcoming rent-seeking behaviour by interest groups. Special interest groups with restricted or delineated membership, such as cartels, trade bodies, unions, or professions, will seek to persuade politicians to deliver policies that favour their members. These policies will rarely be the best outcome for other parts of society, but they have no incentive to organise or lobby against the policies (Olson 1982). Amartya Sen forcefully demonstrated the importance of good politics for a sound economy in his work linking the presence of famine to the absence of democratic voice (Sen 1982). His account of the capabilities necessary for economic development includes political participation (Sen 2009).

So economists are familiar with the importance of understanding institutions and indeed see their own participation in policy institutions as a contribution to overcoming rent-seeking behaviour. There are quite a few examples of the use of economist-centred institutions in government. In addition to independent agencies like central banks and competition authorities, another type is the expert report. Governments frequently commission an independent economist to take an impartial view of the evidence and make policy recommendations. There are many examples, spanning the decades, covering politically contentious areas such as finance, housing, old age care, pensions, taxes. One of the purposes of commissioning reports that are led by highly esteemed economists is that the evidence they assemble and their recommendations will be authoritative and can give the government cover for making some unpopular (with some) decisions—for all policies generally have losers as well as winners. However, the existence of a report does not translate easily or directly into policy. A few hundred pages of careful analysis lack political weight compared to the lobbying efforts of the special interests affected. This can equally derail economic analysis inside government, of course. Powerful lobby groups are—well, powerful.

If interest group pressures make the independent report too weak a political instrument, other institutional embodiments of economic analysis as a counter to rent-seeking have been more effective. In the UK, Royal Commissions in the past typically had enough stature to enable governments to legislate against special interest groups. They are no longer used, though. In contrast, economic regulators have grown in number and are empowered to take decisions more or less independently of the political process, in the general public or consumer interest as set out in statute. Sector regulators are often set up to oversee privatised industries or essential utilities such as electricity and water, to safeguard consumers, although the large economics literature examining regulation warns of the danger of regulatory capture. Financial regulation up to 2008 seems a good example of the reality of this danger. Independent competition regulators, on the other hand, have a good record of countering industry special interests, although the legislation has carved out some exceptions where politicians, perhaps unfortunately, still have the last word. The sectors reserved for politics always include defence. In UK legislation they also include the media and—pushed through against the better judgement of the competition bodies as an emergency measure at the height of the financial crisis—banking. It is hard for bodies regulating important sectors to resist political pressures.

Removing decisions from the hands of politicians can be used to overcome another credibility problem sometimes experienced by governments. Not only is the political process vulnerable to capture by interest groups, it is also prone to capture by impatience, or short-termism. Here the enemy of decisions taken objectively in the general interest is not a special interest group but rather the imperiousness of the present at the expense of the future. Just as today's desire for chocolate cake all too easily outweighs my wish for a smaller waistline tomorrow, politicians will be tempted to reduce interest rates for a faster growth rate now, even knowing that there will be a price to pay in higher inflation tomorrow. As the short-run temptation is obvious, a political pledge to make the virtuous choice every time will not be credible. On the other hand, an independent central bank does not face the same short-run pressures, and indeed can be structured so that its reputation depends on long-term economic outcomes. This could include, for instance, term limits on appointments. Central bank independence has become part of the landscape in democracies, albeit undermined in some eyes by the length and scale of quantitative easing, requiring vast central bank purchases of government bonds. The UK's Office for Budget Responsibility is a more recent institution addressing a credibility problem in commitment to fiscal policy. Other countries have different structures, such as the Congressional Budget Office in the United States, or the Central Planning Bureau (now more accurately self-described as the Bureau for Economic Policy Analysis) in the Netherlands, evaluating political parties' policies.

THE TECHNOCRATIC DILEMMA

Unelected officials in an independent body with a mandate to apply economic analysis can perhaps recommend policies in a more objective way, within a given intellectual framework. Naturally, these independent economic institutions will lack the democratic legitimacy of elected politicians or officials who are directly answerable to, and sackable by, politicians. Daniel Bell identified as long ago as 1973 an emerging political fault-line in the tension between the growing populism of modern democracy in the mass media age and the growing requirement for technical expertise in running a modern economy. In *The Coming of Post-Industrial Society* he predicted that technocrats such as economists, the 'hierophants of the new society', would either align themselves with politicians, or compete with politicians.

This tension approached breaking point in Greece in the aftermath of the GFC, where economist and former central banker Lucas Papademos became prime minister, and in Italy, where economist and former European Commissioner Mario Monti did likewise. Both came to office in 2011, selected by their parliamentarians but at the insistence of EU and IMF leaders, specifically to implement 'structural reforms'. This term is a piece of economics jargon describing policy changes intended to overturn institutions embedding certain interests—such as labour market structures that make hiring young people too expensive. Structural reform is therefore inherently political in the sense that it will pit the interests of some groups in society against others. Although distinct from the wider Eurozone and banking system problems, both the Greek and Italian economies are widely thought to be hamstrung by an accumulation of regulations favouring some groups at the expense of competition, innovation, and economic growth, and thereby the population as a whole. Both technocratic governments faced public discontent and demonstrations in 2012.

In the years since then, the tension between experts and populism has only increased, and not because the technocrats are right and the *vox populi* wrong. It is true both that modern economies are complex, requiring expertise to devise policies, and that, for many people, those policies have not delivered benefits. Looking back from the coronavirus era, with an economic downturn exacerbating and exposing major inequalities, it would be hard to claim that post-GFC economic policies have served the majority well (Algan et al. 2017; Rodrik 2018).

The tension is well illustrated by protests against a specific 'structural reform', the deregulation of taxi markets. Taxi drivers are one of the interest groups most prone to protest— long before Uber disrupted so many cities' taxi markets. For instance, Greek taxi drivers went on strike regularly from July 2011, so the bill to liberalise the taxi trade (part of the reforms required by lenders bailing out the government) was steadily watered down in parliament as elections approached in April 2012. As for Italy, in 2005 the economist Francesco Giavazzi had merely written a newspaper column advocating market reform, but his photograph was circulated to all Milan's cab drivers so they could refuse him as a passenger, and for five nights cabs gathered around his home, sounding their horns through the night (Segal 2012). Mr Monti bravely had another go in 2012, and the taxi drivers did not like it. The *Financial Times* reported:

> Taxi drivers in Rome, among the strongest opponents of liberalisation, are thought to have been instrumental in the 2008 election of Gianni Alemanno, the capital's first

rightwing mayor since the second world war. Mr Monti's proposed reforms, which would have opened up territorial operating restrictions—for example, allowing out-of-town taxi drivers to operate in Rome—were widely welcomed by Romans but duly resisted by Mr Alemanno.

Claudio Giudici, chairman of the Tuscany branch of Uritaxi, the national taxi drivers union, defended their opposition to proposed liberalisation as a 'passionate effort by forces engaged in an actual democratic resistance against the transformation of Italy from a republic into an oligarchical state' (Dinmore 2012).

Mr Giudici was spot on in identifying the paradox, although arguably not in his interpretation of it. The formal institutions of democracy are open to effective lobbying by identifiable groups in their own interest, whereas the technocratic, elite economists are better able than elected politicians to act in the interests of the wider public, by enabling competition and growth. But, as this quotation underlines, technocratic government by economists is itself political. The economist's analytical perspective of benign objectivity, while essential to devising policies in the broad public interest, cannot survive the transition from ivory tower to the streets, or even to the quiet and shabby corridors of regulatory office blocks. Often, economists say of policies such as structural reforms, 'if only the politicians would just do it'. But if a policy is politically impossible to implement, the economic analysis is fundamentally flawed. This is all the more problematic when economists as a profession tend to hold views that many others would consider reflect a particular political stance—in other words, a pro-market instinct—although many economists working on policy areas regard themselves as non-ideological.

THE REDISCOVERY OF POLITICAL ECONOMY

The political nature of policy economics is intensified by the direct demands of politics. If politicians create the demand, some economists will be happy to provide the supply. This may reflect their own politics, as with the minority of UK economists who publicly advocated for Brexit. It is flattering to be asked for advice by somebody close to power. What's more, research funding now comes with a requirement for 'impact', of which the number of encounters with the policy-making world is one important measure. Consultancy firms or investment banks are only too pleased with the PR opportunities provided by their economists' eye-catching interventions in the policy debate. The impact is delivered, the eye of the public is caught, by confident statements of extreme views, rather than by modest or nuanced analyses of complicated situations.

This eagerness to meet a market need makes public policy economics vulnerable to intellectual fashions. Here are two examples, from different eras. One example is 'happiness' economics. Although there are indeed some robust empirical results, such as the correlation between having a job or a stable relationship and individual well-being, the factoid in wide circulation about the lack of correlation between income above a certain level and happiness leads to a conclusion—we don't need further income growth—that is not so well founded. For people with higher incomes consistently report themselves to be happier than those with low incomes, and increases in income are correlated with increased reported happiness (Stevenson and Wolfers 2008). In the world of academic economic research, attention has turned to broader, subtle interdisciplinary questions about the drivers of people's psychological well-being. Nevertheless, campaigning for 'happiness' has a strong afterlife in the public domain, and has a strong appeal to those who distrust economics as being (they think) all about money and profit.

An earlier example dates from the late 1970s and early 1980s, when a revival of classical monetarism combined with the development of rational expectations, 'real business cycle' models of the economy in academic research (that is, business cycles being due only to supply-side shocks such as a new technology). This is the fashion that lured me as a graduate student. There were some good reasons for the intellectual shift then towards what are termed 'microfoundations' for macroeconomic analysis, and the contention that in the short term the economy's (metaphorical) aggregate supply curve was vertical, or in other words, output cannot be increased quickly when demand is rising. The reasons lay in the dismal economic performance of the 1970s, which tested to destruction the previous generation of macroeconomic theories. One consequence was policy monetarism. Macroeconomic policy came to be focused entirely on how fast certain monetary aggregates were growing. In principle, using monetary growth to inform monetary policy is perfectly sensible. In practice, the reality of politics turned it into an obsession with hitting specific monetary growth targets. But they were unattainable because of the deregulation of financial markets and the development of new transactions technologies at exactly the same time, encouraged by the very actions the government was taking to limit monetary growth. This meant there was a shift of unknowable scale in the relationship between monetary growth and the wider economy—the 'velocity' of money, or the number of times it changes hands in a given period, was increasing. The financial deregulation and innovation meant that the economic meaning of any given measure and growth rate of the money supply was unclear.

What's more, the act of using policy levers to target the growth of any specific monetary aggregate also induced changes in people's behaviour that made that aggregate irrelevant for the wider policy aim—in this context, this is known as Goodhart's Law, which states that the act of targeting a variable eliminates the information that made it a useful policy indicator in the first place. As Charles Goodhart expressed it, 'Any observed statistical regularity will tend to collapse once pressure is placed upon it for control purposes' (Goodhart 1975, 122). It is another example of the reflexive nature of economic policy analysis discussed above.

Nevertheless, the government of the day clung on to monetary growth targets for some years. My job as a very junior economist in the Treasury in 1985–86 included the dull task of constructing a variety of new monetary aggregates and calculating which had the slowest growth rate. This slower-growing new measure (named PSLX in my computer programme) joined the earlier official targets in the next Budget, although it also subsequently joined them in their unwelcome exuberance. It lived up to Goodhart's Law, as its growth accelerated as soon as it became an official policy target (renamed PSL2).

The point of this anecdote is that the refraction of an intellectual trend in academic economics through the political process sometimes leads to a set of ideas being too dominant and too long-lived in the policy world after the academic bandwagon has rolled on. And, of course, there are some economists with an ideological agenda, either left or right of centre. If they can, they will influence policy accordingly.

Finally, once ideas get into the policy and political process, they develop an institutional life of their own. People's jobs are shaped around them, funding is secured, statistics are collected, monthly meetings set up, journalists are briefed. It becomes

embarrassing to abandon a policy, given what political opponents and the media will make of it—the fear of U-turns is
extreme.

The inseparability of economics and politics is most directly
obvious in the case of macroeconomic policy. It is not all that
long—the early 2000s—since macroeconomics was triumphant.
There was a strong consensus among macroeconomists about
how the economy operated and how it should be managed
through fiscal and monetary policy, described as the 'new neoclassical synthesis'. This was believed to have brought about the
'Great Moderation', over a decade of low inflation and steady
growth. The role of sheer luck in bringing about the Great Moderation was, as it turns out, greatly underestimated. Few macroeconomists were keen to admit that the GFC of 2008 significantly damaged their subject, which is perhaps not surprising.
Some, moreover, engaged in confident arguments over fiscal
and monetary policy in the media and blogosphere, as if calls in
the aftermath of the GFC for economists to show more humility
had fallen on deaf ears—it became known as the debate between
saltwater (departments like Harvard on the US East Coast) and
freshwater (Chicago on Lake Michigan) schools. This debate
between competing anti- and pro-austerity schools in the 2010s
was eerily similar to the Keynesian versus monetarist arguments
of the equally crisis-ridden late 1970s, when I started my career
in economics. Should western governments be engaging in budget austerity or in Keynesian stimulus? Is the current recession
different in kind from one that does not result from a banking
crisis? Should there be more quantitative easing or not? One
can find more than one answer to each of these questions in
the macro literature.

When macroeconomists have such directly opposing views,
held so strongly and expressed so bitterly on social media and

blogs, we are far from the realm of hard science and evidently do not know the answers. It is equally clear that any given macroeconomist's views about macroeconomic policy are often a good predictor of their political views, and perhaps the converse is also true. It is not even clear to me that there is any prospect of answering all the important macro questions of our day by the usual econometric methods, as it is inherently difficult to identify what causes what in the complex, dynamic environment of a modern economy. History is just as important as economics in this section of the toolbox, in order to untangle causal links and identify policy opportunities.

Macroeconomists to whom I have expressed this opinion strongly disagree. They point to specific macroeconomic models that have not been challenged in theory and have been vindicated empirically. They argue that the profession gave good advice in the aftermath of the crisis, saving us from another Great Depression. Conventional international macro models can explain a lot about the origins of the 2012 Eurozone crisis, and indeed many macroeconomists predicted the non-viability of the euro before its launch, including those at the UK Treasury (HM Treasury 2003). The fact that macroeconomic policy since 2008 has avoided the policy errors of the 1930s is further evidence that macroeconomics has progressed, and many macroeconomists would argue that the pre-crisis models have been made considerably richer by adding, for example, financial intermediation and imperfect competition. Certainly there has been a large amount of impressive work in macroeconomics in the years since 2008–9.

But to my mind this does not fundamentally change the picture of a profound lack of consensus about how the economy as a whole functions and therefore what policies will make it function better. The schism was vigorously expressed in a famous, or perhaps notorious, article by Paul Krugman, somebody who is a master of the art of polemic in economics. He wrote, referring to leading American academics:

> [I]n the wake of the crisis, the fault lines in the economics profession have yawned wider than ever. [Robert] Lucas says the Obama administration's stimulus plans are 'schlock economics,' and his Chicago colleague John Cochrane says they're based on discredited 'fairy tales'. In response, Brad DeLong of the University of California, Berkeley, writes of the 'intellectual collapse' of the Chicago School, and I myself have written that comments from Chicago economists are the product of a Dark Age of macroeconomics in which hard-won knowledge has been forgotten (Krugman 2006).

The consequences have been regrettable. Simon Wren-Lewis noted that macroeconomists argue now for their 'school of thought' rather than on the merits of the case. He adds: 'I also miss the synthesis. I very much liked the idea that disagreements could be clearly located within a common framework. With the synthesis, I felt macroeconomics began to look more like a unified discipline—more like micro, and dare I say it, more like a science than a belief system' (Wren-Lewis 2012b). Has this changed between 2012 and the pandemic? Controversy has raged about 'Modern Monetary Theory', which seems to me as an outsider to macroeconomics to be a continuation of the Keynesian-Monetarist and Saltwater-Freshwater splits. There has certainly been strong majority opinion about the right kinds of fiscal and monetary policy to apply during this Covid19 crisis. But I am not persuaded—more on this in Chapter Two.

Macroeconomics is not only what many people (mistakenly) think all economists do; it is indeed an important part of what policy economists actually do. Most macroeconomists work either for the government and central banks or in financial markets. There is no escape from the need to work on the basis of some reasoned assumptions about the near future (forecasts, as they are called, although 'conditional projections' would be more accurate). The comparison with weather forecasting is often made—another imprecise science, once marked by bitter arguments about the right analytical framework for understanding the climate as a whole, but essential for the planning of everyday life. Although the uncertainty attached to weather forecasts is widely understood, economic forecasts are often—wrongly—regarded by the general public as more certain, not least because of the way some economists at any rate talk about them. Macroeconomic forecasters need to be more explicit about uncertainty (and many are), as do the journalists who report their work (not so much). There are other lessons to be taken from the groupthink that prevented so many economists from seeing clearly enough or communicating effectively enough the risks in obvious precursors of trouble in the early 2000s, such as persistent current account imbalances and the build-up of debt. These lessons would include paying more attention to economic history, to institutional realities (such as the changing character of the financial system in the 1990s and 2000s including the growth of 'shadow' banking and high frequency trading), and perhaps a greater pluralism in the practice of macroeconomics.

It is not only in the case of macroeconomics, though, that political opinions can be elided with economic conclusions. Economics has plenty of territory where the truth is not known, or at least not yet, or needs to be carefully expressed. But politics and nuance are strangers. Even when there is a professional consensus about certain empirical results, controversy can rage over their interpretation or implications, especially when one political party has staked a claim to certain policies. One example would be research looking at the effects of competition in the English National Health Service on health outcomes. There is consistent evidence from three large studies now that some forms of competition in the provision of services have positive effects (albeit with important caveats, for example, about the risk of private entrants to the market cherry picking the easiest patients, and including a lack of support in the results for price rather than quality competition). This conclusion proved simply unacceptable to, among others, the editors of *The Lancet*, who published an ad hominem attack by medical researchers on the economists. The economists were given a right of reply in the journal only reluctantly (Bloom et al. 2011). There will be many more controversies of this kind in the new age of populism. The domain of solid empirical knowledge will continue to expand slowly but the border between soundly-based professional consensus and conjecture, which is bound to be influenced by political beliefs, is both hazy and shifting.

The fact that economists and non-economists have a different set of prior beliefs about some fundamental economic issues will only enhance the scope for discord on specific areas of policy. Whether because of their self-selection into a subject that appeals to them or because their training shapes their thinking so forcefully, economists on average are more favourable than the wider population to market forces as a mechanism for improving the public good, free trade, and so on. David Henderson forcefully criticised what he labelled (in the 1985 BBC Reith Lectures) 'do-it-yourself' economics.[13] He was

13. http://www.bbc.co.uk/programmes/p00gq1cr/episodes/player, accessed 17 April 2012.

referring to what the layperson takes as common sense but the economist knows to be untrue. One example concerns trade, where the common sense view is that exports are good and imports bad. To the typical economist it is, if anything, the other way around, and problems arise only if there is a very large and persistent surplus in either direction. Comparative advantage is another unintuitive concept, yet specialisation on the basis of comparative advantage and trade can deliver large mutual benefits (as well as always-destabilising disruption). Specialisation and exchange, either domestic or international, are the source of the transformative economic growth of the past quarter millennium. They are the drivers of the global supply chains now under attack for reasons of national advantage or resilience during a crisis. Common sense finds it equally hard to accept that jobs have no objective existence in the economy separate from the people who currently do them (the 'lump of labour fallacy'), or that it can be a good thing for the economy's growth rate if some businesses are allowed to fail. Applied economists have a pragmatic common language for assembling evidence and discussing policy. Disagreements concern the details of empirical methods or the interpretation of evidence. This is normal science at work. But many lay people or indeed politicians will not like the results, if these contradict their prior beliefs.

On the other hand, there is a lot that economists do not know and yet some over-claim for. There are economists commenting on public policy who are ideologues and are not engaged in the detailed work of expanding empirical knowledge in specific contexts. It is understandably hard to back away from strong claims, all the harder the more confidently they are made. One of the reasons that specific policies survive for a long time, arguably well past their use-by date, is the difficulty for politicians and their advisers of appearing to make a U-turn in a democracy with a cynical media. To the extent that we join in the cynicism, we all help to sustain the inability of the political and policy process to be adaptable to either new evidence or the evolution of economic knowledge. However, the interaction between economics and politics and media means that policy economists all too often end up expressing certainty where they are actually most uncertain—in those areas where economics is most divided and least well-founded on careful and consistent empirical evidence. This is perhaps more often the case with economists who work outside government but are trying to influence policy. Think tankers and media commentators are particularly prone to this kind of humility-bypass, despite the many cautionary tales furnished by the experience of the GFC.

Yet economists in government and the academic world are probably too diffident about insisting on what we can say with reasonable confidence in many areas of policy. Some people do so perfectly cheerfully, especially when it comes to debunking policy fads or zombie ideas that stagger around Whitehall, but there are too few economists who bother to jump into the bear pit of public debate. This is entirely understandable because nuance dies in this arena. The media, online comment, and political reaction can be brutal. Even worse, for some academic researchers, their results can be hijacked to serve a political purpose. Elected governments have also won a mandate to ignore expert advice if they like, although in recent decades they have limited their ability to do so by setting up the economic institutions that operate more or less independently.

But I firmly believe economists could, and should, play a greater role in explaining the consequences of some choices. Given that we as a profession collectively, and cheerfully, repeat some unpopular truths, such as the merits of trade or the importance of competition rather than government control of markets, it is odd that we hold back from unpopularity across the whole spectrum of what we think we know with reasonable confidence. Even then, it is engagement in the debate that is important. There is a new interest in what is described as the public understanding of economics, but to my mind it needs to be a conversation, not a lecture.

THE PUBLIC RESPONSIBILITIES OF THE ECONOMIST

Economics plays an important, an essential, role in public policy. Its status is well-deserved. The majority of economists involved in policy research today are pragmatists with a shared set of data and tools for discovering incremental policy improvements. Economists continue to regard markets as the best, although imperfect, means of allocating resources, and continue to assume that people respond to incentives according to a more or less well-founded assessment of their own interests. But these beliefs are not merely an act of faith. They are increasingly well grounded in evidence and experience. People who choose to do applied policy economics are often motivated by a strong inner drive to help tackle social ills such as poverty, unemployment, and ignorance. The number of economists who are ideologically opposed to government intervention at all is minuscule—those who are tend to be located somewhere in the deeply divided United States.

Economics brings a kind of toughness of thought to policy-making, through insisting on thinking about opportunity costs, the balance of costs and benefits, and the likelihood that people will respond to incentives. Institutions employing economists to give technocratic advice can be used as counterweights to powerful interest group lobbies, or as commitment devices to limit political short-termism.

So in a number of ways, policy economics has proven its worth. However, it also has important failings. Above all, economists do not pay enough attention to their own political and institutional role in the policy process. It is not that there is no awareness of it at all. There are specific instances where it is explicitly discussed, such as the acknowledgement of 'regulatory capture', the phenomenon of time inconsistency, and the contribution of central banks to limiting the 'political business cycle'. However, policy economists do not extend this self-knowledge and reflexivity as far as they should, to acknowledge that they are themselves agents in the decision-making processes they are modelling. The result is a certain naïvety about how expert research, or technocratic advice, will be implemented and how people will respond.

The public responsibilities of the economist can be summed up as follows:

- Be brave about your conclusions when they are based on sound empirical research;
- Be simultaneously modest about your conclusions, and own up to the limits of knowledge and the nature of uncertainty;
- Do not hold back from public debate about controversial subjects;
- But if you are arguing on the basis of your political views rather than empirical research, or taking a view that supports a particular company or interest that has been funding your research, you have a duty to say so;
- Above all, communicate better with non-economists and the general public, because good economic policies will not be implemented if they do not have popular legitimacy, and the public understanding of economics is low.

I end up with the sense that in what we collectively say about public policy, economists generally sound too certain where we ought to be humble, and too hesitant where we ought to have more confidence. The imperative driving these behaviours may be the natural wish to tell others engaged in policy-making what they want to hear. But if you want to be liked, you probably should not become an economist.

The main point of this chapter, though, is the need to think about ourselves as participants in society, while retaining the worthy ambition to act as impartially as possible in the general public interest. This is needed in the specifics of policy analysis, where it could avert at least some examples of 'government failure': any intervention will cause a reaction, and that needs to be part of the analysis. But it is above all needed in the sense of economists engaged with policy about political economy, not economics. It is commonplace to say this is a populist era. In most western economies people have become more polarised, for reasons ranging from the effects of social media to the failure of some people and places to experience economic improvements. In these kinds of times, to be a technocrat is to be a political agent. Insisting to a protesting public that one really has their best interests at heart is not a persuasive stance.

Intermission

The year I delivered the Tanner Lectures in Oxford, on which Chapter One builds, was a busy one for me. I had been thinking about the themes in the chapter for a year or so. Around the same time in 2011–12 a number of conversations with fellow economists fed concerns, not only those preoccupations about the role of economists in society and policy, and the need to do a better job of engaging in public debate, but also concerns about the undergraduate curriculum. After all, people who go on to work as economists, or just vote on the basis of economic policy platforms, started out as our students. Were we at fault for the narrowness and lack of perspective of the profession because of what and how we taught? That was the tentative conclusion I drew from private discussions. What could I—then in a half-time public service role as vice chair of the BBC Trust and half-time running a small consultancy—do?

I went to speak to Andy Ross, then a UK Treasury economist and senior figure in the Government Economic Service (GES). He leapt at my suggestion of a conference bringing together employers of economists and academics responsible for teaching economics in Britain's universities. The GES and Bank of England sponsored the conference, hosted at the Bank in February 2012. We need not have been nervous about filling the 120-capacity lecture theatre there; the event was over-subscribed. We had struck a nerve, among employers and teachers alike, with participants from investment banks and major companies as well as the public sector employers of new graduates, and many academics from around the country. Employers consistently said their new recruits were technically highly adept but knew no recent economic history and were unable to communicate with non-specialists. As one said, 'I don't expect new graduates to be fully-baked but I don't expect them to be half-baked either.'

One reason for the interest among the academics present was the emergence in the previous year or two of student protests about the content and character of what they were being taught in their undergraduate degrees. One active, high-profile group was the University of Manchester's Post-Crash Economics Society, some of whose enthusiastic and talented members I either taught or worked with when I took up a chair at Manchester in 2014. Another was the group Rethinking Economics. Although committed students were at the forefront, protest about economics was very much in the air, post-GFC. The Institute for New Economic Thinking had been founded in 2010, with an inaugural conference at Cambridge linking the economic crisis with a crisis in economics.[1] The 'Post-Autistic Economics' movement had emerged in France even prior to the GFC.[2] Although some mainstream economists were defen-

1. https://www.ineteconomics.org/events/the-economic-crisis-and-the-crisis-in-economics.
2. http://www.paecon.net/HistoryPAE.htm.

sive, it was undeniable that many economics courses ignored the most cataclysmic economic event in recent memory, and failed to teach students about the exciting—and real-world-relevant—economics at the frontiers of research, in applied areas students care about such as inequality or climate change.

One of the speakers at our Bank of England and GES conference was Wendy Carlin of University College, London, a leading UK macroeconomist.[3] She, with Sam Bowles of the University of Massachusetts at Amherst, had begun to work on an ambitious initiative to reshape the entire first year undergraduate curriculum by providing a new and better one that would be freely available online, and persuading universities around the world to adopt it. Wendy and Sam had been inspired by students, not only in the UK but elsewhere in the world, particularly Chile. The new curriculum—now CORE's The Economy—would teach theory as a means of understanding real-world economic issues, would embed an appreciation of politics, power, and institutions, and would provide history, including the history of economic thought, as well as the usual technical tools.[4] Exciting areas of research from environmental economics to inequality to innovation and digital competition would not be shoved into the final chapter of a textbook, never to be reached. I was one of the many volunteer co-authors from around the world of the new curriculum. It had been adopted (by fall 2019) by 271 universities in 53 countries, and translated into several languages. CORE (of which I was also a trustee for several years) had also produced an online programme for

3. The contributions were written up and published as Coyle (ed.), 2012.

4. coreecon, n.d., 'The Economy', https://www.core-econ.org/project/core-the -economy/.

non-specialists who are interested in economics and started to reach into high schools.

Questioning students, and the visible efforts of many colleagues to bring about improvements in economics courses, have had a broader effect. Very few universities have failed to change what they teach. At Harvard, the famous Ec 10 introductory course long taught by Greg Mankiw was refreshed in 2019 by new course leaders, Jason Furman and David Laibson, not least in the light of student dissatisfaction.[5] Harvard also introduced in 2019 a new course, likely to be an inspiration for other universities, 'Using Big Data to Solve Economic and Social Problems', taught by Raj Chetty.[6] None of this is to say that there is nothing left to improve. There has, though, been much change since I gave the Pro Bono Economics lecture in 2013, from which this next chapter draws.[7] I was immersed in the early stages of my contribution to CORE, alongside chairing a Royal Economic Society steering group on teaching economics.[8] So the shortcomings of macroeconomics raised by the financial crisis were much on my mind.

5. Editorial, 'Ec 10 Shifts to the Future', *The Harvard Crimson*, 4 April 2019, https://www.thecrimson.com/article/2019/4/4/editorial-ec-10-shifts-future/.

6. Dylan Matthews, 'The Radical Plan to Change How Harvard Teaches Economics', *Vox,* 22 May 2019, https://www.vox.com/the-highlight/2019/5/14/18520783/harvard-economics-chetty.

7. https://www.probonoeconomics.com/news/pbe-lecture-2013-diane-coyle.

8. 'Teaching Economics after the Crisis', Royal Economic Society, 1 April 2013, https://www.res.org.uk/resources-page/april-2013-newsletter-teaching-economics-after-the-crisis.html.

2

The Economist as Outsider

The previous chapter discussed the perspective economists take when we are evaluating a policy or intervention. It argued that too often we present ourselves as outsiders, looking down objectively on human societies. But that is not how society sees us. This claim to impartial outsider status indeed weakens economics, as it sounds like self-interest. Like the protagonist of Albert Camus' great novel, *L'Étranger*, we are discovering that it is not possible to be disengaged from society. Economics has to reconnect—and it can do so.

When I say 'we', I do not just mean 'I', but a large number of academic and professional economists who, not surprisingly, have been re-evaluating the subject since 2008, and in the UK again since 2016. Most students doing economics degrees will not become economists; most of those who do will work in business or in public service. One of their main tasks will be assessing the impact of policy changes or other interventions. Many employers have expressed concern about the narrowness of the economists they hire. The complaints in the post-GFC years were consistent. Employers said they could hire graduates who were technically very able and could manipulate models, but who were wholly unable to apply what they had learned in any real-world context, did not have practical data skills, were unable to communicate with non-specialists, were unaware of context or recent economic history, and had not been taught any of the new, policy-relevant areas of economics, particularly the behavioural findings. As well as the energetic student-driven reform movement, there was tremendous public interest in the economy—an evident passion to understand the world in uncertain times, and a sense that events had seriously tested economics. The interest has only grown. As the pandemic-related lockdowns have continued, the appetite for discussion about what kind of economic recovery is desirable, and whether GDP growth is a good target, is apparent.

So wanting to see change in economics is not a fringe or 'heterodox' agenda. Nor is it just a question of changing the curriculum, or the academic research agenda, for the future; it is also about the kind of impact assessment work undertaken widely in public policy and consultancies. Nor is it hard to identify some desirable changes, although inevitably harder to implement them. There has been some progress during the past decade but there is certainly further to go.

Madness in Our Methodology

There is a particular way in which economics often does seem to care more about logical rigour than reality, despite the apparently increasingly desperate attempts by reality to get economists to pay attention. Imagine yourself in an academic seminar in an economics department. The conventions of behaviour here seem to allow for aggressive treatment of colleagues—as noted in the Introduction, the subject has a serious culture problem—and one of the participants is hunting for the most damning adjective he can find to describe the paper he has just heard presented. He settles on 'ad hoc'. To describe an economic model as 'ad hoc' is to dismiss it, in a damning way.

What does this insult mean? Economists put models at the heart of their methodology. A model is an attempt to make sense of the world by including only relevant detail. A good model is a powerful tool for analysis and prediction. As mentioned in Chapter One, one well-known example of a good model is the map of the London Underground originally developed by Harry Beck. It is a flawed guide, for example, taking tourists down two deep escalators, to wait on the platform and travel 260 meters on a train, and then up in a lift, if they want to travel from Leicester Square to Covent Garden. This is a three-minute walk above ground. Still, the map is an accurate enough representation of London's geography for its purpose and an invaluable guide for passengers. Its combination of reasonably accurate analysis, parsimonious representation and sheer elegance makes it a model model.

However, many economic models fall short of the Tube map standard. Most often, their failure is one of inaccuracy by over-simplification. Economists value logic, parsimony, and elegance—sometimes more than reality—and like an academic paper to have some impressive algebra to express the logic. I have been asked by journal editors to insert some equations that say in algebra the same as the surrounding words. The linguistic philosopher Alfred Korzybski (1933) famously warned against believing too much in a model: 'The map is not the territory.' The aim in modelling should be finding a happy medium: between navigating around London only via Tube; and making the opposite error of piling on descriptive detail without any analytical abstraction in a kind of Borgesian paradox where the entire territory is the only possible map (Borges 1975 [1946]).

The economist who accommodates reality, by using rules of thumb with no 'microfoundations'—meaning theoretical accounts of actions at the level of every individual—will often be criticised for ad hoc-ery by their peers. Algebra or 'math' is essential in empirical work; it enforces logic and enables the use of applied statistical techniques in a rigorous way. But at the same time academic economics is overly fond of models expressed in terms of algebra or calculus (really, logic statements) embodying such microfoundations. There are many papers in the journals with masses of equations which end up proving what they assume in setting up the algebra of the model. Paul Romer, no slouch at the mathematics, has criticised this predilection as 'mathiness'. Above all many models built on supposedly rigorous microfoundations can be ad hoc too: they are ad hoc with respect to evidence, though, rather than with respect to logic.

Take game theory, rightly considered to be one of the jewels in the crown of the discipline. It models formally how people behave in strategic situations, where what one person chooses to do will depend on what the others do, and these decisions can play out over time. The standard assumption is that the players choose rationally: they will calculate what is in their best interests, given their assumption that everyone else will do the same. This is the Nash equilibrium concept. Nobody can do any better by taking a different course of action. Game theory has been successfully applied in practical contexts ranging from business strategy to spectrum auctions, with excellent results.

Ariel Rubinstein has experimented with specific games, or strategic contests, with his students, audiences at his lectures, and respondents to his website surveys, collecting more than

13,000 responses altogether. His conclusion is that people do not behave in life as they are assumed to do in game-theoretic models. Relatively few end up at the Nash equilibrium outcome predicted by theory. More opt for 'naïve' solutions that don't take any account at all of how others might respond. More still show signs of thinking strategically but getting the calculation wrong. Rubinstein points out that if you are rational and can do the calculations, then playing the game on the assumption that others are doing the same will in fact leave you worse off than assuming that they will act naïvely or capriciously. Those who have learnt some game theory are more likely to choose the Nash equilibrium answer, which is in reality incorrect: 'A small group of students had internalized the ideas presented in a game theory course, even choosing the equilibrium point when this wasn't really the intelligent thing to do' (Rubenstein 2012, 111). Or at least, not the intelligent thing to do if their aim was to maximise the amount of money they made. People playing games, whether in the lecture hall or in life, might have other aims such as harmonious social relationships that make their seemingly unintelligent or irrational choices perfectly reasonable.

For the word 'rational' is ambiguous. Economists mean 'logically consistent'. Normal people often mean 'reasonable' instead. Daniel Kahneman and other cognitive scientists have shown that generally economic rationality has to be learnt (Kahneman 2011). Steven Pinker has pointed out that humans did not evolve to think about numbers and find calculation hard, and that, 'The logic of the market is cognitively unnatural' (Pinker 2007). The default assumption in economics remains that humans think in the 'slow' way, making logical calculations; but this is energy-intensive and tiring, and we economise on it. It may sometimes be correct, and is a reasonable starting point, but needs to be tested in given contexts. In some cases, 'ad hoc' models will be empirically more realistic.

What's more, maximisation (of a firm's profits or of an individual's utility) is neutral about goals, even goals that have what many consider to be obviously undesirable consequences. Thus people's decisions about smoking, or marriage and children, or crime, are assessed wholly through the prism of utility maximisation, like any other consumer choice. Nobel laureate Gary Becker started the tradition of applying the standard economic mode of analysis to decisions generally not considered as 'economic', in family and social life. Economists think this is normal, having become habituated to it. Others do not. As one comment in *Scientific American* put it, 'Though this has method, yet there is madness in it' (Bhalla 2013).

Economics is, of course, steadily embracing the behavioural findings of psychologists and cognitive scientists. It is surely also time for economists to start incorporating other motivations—'non-economic' motivations—into our models, as well as cognitively-realistic modes of choice. These can include altruism and pro-social motivations (Bowles 2016), or a sense of identity, honour, duty, or patriotism. Others pose a significant challenge to basic microeconomic analysis. For example, people do not have fixed preferences, as in the canonical consumer choice model, but are strongly affected by social norms, or advertising. This makes the framework of individual utility maximisation rather doubtful, as it assumes fixed preferences known to the individual. Yet in this theoretical world, advertising would not work and impulse purchases could not occur.

Some economists incorporate social influences on choice in their work, such as Ed Glaeser, in his research on 'non-market' phenomena such as crime waves or obesity (Glaeser and

Scheinkman 2000). George Akerlof and Rachel Kranton look at people's decisions from the perspective of personal identity:

> Men and women in the United States smoked cigarettes at vastly different rates at the beginning of the twentieth century, but these rates largely converged by the 1980s. Women now smoke just as much as men. We cannot explain this convergence in terms of standard economic arguments, such as changes in relative prices and incomes, because no such changes were sufficiently large. But we can explain it if we ask how people think about themselves—that is, if we examine changes in gender norms. Women early in the twentieth century were not supposed to smoke; it was inappropriate behavior. By the 1970s, however, advertising campaigns targeted 'liberated' women, telling them that smoking was not only acceptable, but desirable (Akerlof and Kranton 2010).

All in all, there is overwhelming evidence that the construct of rational economic man is wrong in certain circumstances; it is not even valid in the 'as if' way, famously introduced as a defence of *homo economicus* by Milton Friedman (1966).

Of course, many economists acknowledge the importance of incorporating into their models assumptions about decision making that bear a closer relation to how people do in fact make decisions. This is the behavioural economics revolution, which moved quite quickly from the research lab and seminar room to the corridors of power, and implementation in policies. Another sign that economists and economic policy-makers are embracing different approaches is the enthusiasm for randomised control trials (RCTs) and field experiments. Often linked with behavioural models, these methods started in the development context but are quickly migrating to other areas of policy. The idea is that trials and experiments, if properly constructed, with participants randomly assigned to a treatment or control group, will provide robust evidence of 'what works'. For anybody keen to assess the impact of a policy or intervention, this combination of psychological realism and rigorous method looks unassailable. The approach allows realism without being describable as 'ad hoc', although its generalisability is contested (Deaton 2020). Economists may have become over-enthusiastic about a method when no single method can encapsulate everything we might want to know.

But the economist's typical habit of reductionism dies hard. Paradoxically, the demand for economic advice to be well-founded on the basis of evidence may be feeding this reductionism. Economists are eager to tell everyone 'what works'. Unfortunately, interpreting economic evidence is not a simple business. We are typically trying to test hypotheses about a small number of variables in a complex world of millions of variables, with a huge amount of two-way feedback or simultaneity, and using a relatively small amount of data, sometimes of dubious quality. It is difficult in the extreme to establish causality rather than correlation. Neither RCTs nor more realistic assumptions in economic models make a difference to the sheer difficulty of the empirical challenge. Nate Silver writes in his bestseller *The Signal and the Noise*:

> The government produces data on literally 45,000 economic indicators each year. Private data providers track as many as four million statistics. The temptation that some economists succumb to is to put all this data into a blender and claim that the resulting gruel is haute cuisine. If you have a statistical model that seeks to explain eleven outputs but has to choose from among four million inputs to do so, many of the relationships it identifies are going to be spurious (Silver 2012).

Econometricians, those economists specialising in applied statistics, know well the risk of over-fitting of economic models, the temptation to prefer inaccurate precision to the accurate imprecision that would more properly characterise noisy data. However, claiming to have discovered causal relationships is a kind of holy grail for empirical economists, and claiming causal findings is made almost irresistible by the allure of finding statistical significance—although it has long been pointed out that this is not always, or often, meaningful (Leamer 1983; Ziliak and McCloskey 2008), and that often when researchers think they have established causality using clever methods, they have not (Ioannides 2017; Young 2017). Unfortunately, a few economics journals that are gatekeepers to the best academic jobs in effect require 'mathiness' and incentivise the hunt for statistical significance. There is a risk that the useful new tool of RCTs could similarly fall victim to over-enthusiasm for 'hard' technique. Trials and experiments, like other empirical methods, need to be done with due humility in the face of our epistemological uncertainty about the world. Whatever the choice of technique, some economists are alarmingly eager to claim an empirical silver bullet delivering firm cause-and-effect recommendations—what policy lever will deliver which outcomes?

In a thoughtful blog post about the appetite among policymakers for evidence of economic impact, Duncan Green of Oxfam wrote that the demand means that:

> The aid business insists on pursuing a linear model of change, either explicitly, or implicitly because a 'good' funding application has a clear set of activities, outputs, outcomes and a 'monitoring, evaluation and learning' system can attribute any change to the project's activities—a highly linear approach. . . .

In denying complexity, one is obliged either to seek islands of linearity in a complex system (vaccines, bed nets), which may not always be the most useful or effective places to engage, or to lie—writing up project reports to turn the experience of 'making it up as you go along' that epitomises working in complex systems into the magical world of linear project implementation, 'roll out', 'best practice' and all the rest (Oxfam 2013).

This even though a society or economy is a complex, non-linear system with multiple feedbacks and two-way causality (Colander and Kupers 2014). The moral applies in all areas of applied economics, not just the aid business seeking ways to stimulate economic development in low-income countries.

I draw two conclusions from the temptation to reductionism and cause-and-effect simplifications in much applied economics.

One is that economists need to rely less on models alone, and to embrace theoretical ad-hoc-ery if it seems useful. We have all been trained to love the analytical muscle of the discipline, and of course it is essential to have a theory or hypothesis to test empirically. Nevertheless, we need to supplement the analysis more with narrative approaches, both from economic history and the qualitative methods of other social sciences such as anthropology and sociology. The combination of tools could add up to a more powerful approach to causal evaluation.

Evidence consists of more than data or statistics. It does not even have to be quantifiable. There's a saying that the plural of anecdote is not data. I used to think this was witty. Now I am not so sure. Statistics shed a powerful light in a narrow focus. We do not have statistics on the value of intangible activities such as building apps or consuming online data; Michael Mandel has pointed out the absurdity that official statistics suggest American internet use was making a negative contribution to GDP growth during the period when fixed and mobile broadband subscriptions and usage were exploding (Mandel 2012). Similarly absurd is the large contribution financial services apparently made to UK GDP growth in the final quarter of 2008 (Coyle 2014). The fact that they are not counted does not mean that intangibles are not valuable, no more than the fact that it is counted makes speculative finance valuable. Likewise, social capital is hard to measure, but its importance is clear in social and economic outcomes. Nature provides vast but largely uncounted services to the economy. Some things of value are not only non-monetary but unquantifiable, such as freedom or citizenship.

We economists should concentrate on our comparative advantage in analysis and empirical measurement, but we should also be prepared to supplement it including with an acknowledgement of the unquantifiable. Dani Rodrik summed it up this way: 'To become a true economist, you need to do all sorts of reading . . . that you are never required to do as a student' (Rodrik 2013). Employers of young economists outside academia are keen for graduates to have a far greater awareness of economic history, current conjuncture and political context. Anybody engaged in policy advice or consultancy or advising financial clients knows from experience that there is a world beyond the models.

My second conclusion is that too many economists are just not good enough, or perhaps not modest enough, about the kind of empirical work generally done.

One frequent mistake is a failure to test hypotheses against a specific counterfactual or alternative hypothesis. Less often found in academic research, an example is the kind of economic consultancy research summarised in a *Financial Times* article

(Taylor 2013). It reported that premium headphone-maker Sennheiser was leading a campaign against fake consumer electronics. This is understandable; as a spokesman pointed out, if people buy cheap rip-offs thinking they're the real thing, it will damage the company's reputation. But Sennheiser claimed economic analysis had shown fakes cost them at least $2m a year (equivalent to about one seventh of that year's net profits) in lost sales. Not so. This sum was based on a comparison with the false counterfactual that everyone who bought fake headphones would have bought the real thing if the cheap copy had been unavailable. The true counterfactual is that almost nobody who bought the fake item would have otherwise bought the real one, which costs around $300. If anybody suffered lost sales, it was makers of genuine cheap headphones, who should be joining Sennheiser's campaign. Similarly, almost nobody who buys a $20 'Louis Vuitton' handbag at the local market would otherwise have spent $2000 on the real thing. I suspect that relatively few people who buy fake consumer goods actually think they're getting the real item. The price contains information about authenticity, as most people understand.

The point of the example is that economists must always be clear about counterfactuals. This is fundamental in competition analysis and in good business economics—including estimating the effect of introducing a low-priced copy of a consumer good into a market—and I hope it is now taught in all econometrics courses. Yet even when a counterfactual or alternative hypothesis is explicitly considered, many economists will fall into the trap (described with typical clarity by Ronald Coase, as noted in Chapter One) of comparing a policy with 'an abstract model of a market situation. . . . Unless we realise we are choosing between social situations which are all more or less failures, we will not make much headway.' In other words, to evaluate a policy, realistic counterfactuals must be the point of comparison; otherwise the assessment is no more than what Coase described as 'blackboard economics' (Williams and Coase 1964).

There are embarrassingly many examples of poor empirical work in economics, including over-claiming causality and significance and ignoring the statistical power of results. The econometrics taught to young economists has always been strong on probability theory but in general weaker at preparing them for the pitfalls in handling real data. Perhaps this is changing, although my impression is that too little attention is still paid to the epistemological status of the data it is now so easy to download and feed into statistics packages. Bayesian inference is rarely (though increasingly) taught despite its usefulness as a practical tool in the face of uncertainty. Economics research is hardly ever replicated, nor are negative results published—problems affecting other disciplines too, of course, as the recent 'p-hacking' debate shows (Fanelli 2010; Head et al. 2015). This may be coming for us soon.

One of the improvements employers have long wanted to see in economics degrees is much better practical preparation for collecting and understanding statistics, as well as using them in careful econometrics. This is an area where much has improved in teaching practice in the past decade. A big remaining issue, though, is that many economists are remarkably uncurious about statistics—how they are constructed and adjusted, and how that might limit the conclusions they can support—and still remarkably cavalier about making strong claims on the basis of econometrics taught in too mechanical a way. Participants in seminars obsess about specifics of econometric technique establishing claims to causality; a colleague of mine refers to them as 'the identification police', demanding to know how the author of a paper has 'identified' the true causal relationships. Controversially, perhaps, I do not believe causality can ever be established econometrically. Knowledge from other sources is always needed. These issues of practical data handling will become even more important in the age of big data (Athey 2017).

Going even further out on a limb, macroeconomists seem to me the biggest offenders in not taking such empirical issues seriously enough. This might sound like sheer contrarianism given that macroeconomists are constantly wielding data; after all, their business is analysing the behaviour of the whole economy and forecasting its future path. My concerns are, first, that too few think about the vast uncertainty associated with the statistics they download and use; and, secondly, how difficult it is to draw definitive conclusions about economy-wide phenomena, the aggregated outcomes of choice made by millions of businesses and consumers interacting in specific historical and geographic contexts, and social and political relations. In the immediate aftermath of the financial crisis, there were many calls—from economists—for economists to demonstrate greater humility. David Colander presented a suggestion for a code of ethics to the ASSA meetings in 2011 with the title 'Creating Humble Economists' (Colander 2011). Colander wrote:

> Back in 1927, Lionel Robbins argued that, 'What precision economists can claim at this stage is largely a sham precision. In the present state of knowledge, the man who can claim for economic science much exactitude is a quack.' Despite the advances economic science has made, that remains true today. Yet, all too often economists allow lay people and policy makers to believe that our policy suggestions have far more scientific foundation than a neutral objective observer would give them.

Yet macroeconomists typically draw on a limited range of highly aggregated, correlated, and auto-correlated data, now readily available online, without reflecting enough on how the data have been constructed, to make sometimes strong claims. Indeed, Carmen Reinhart and Ken Rogoff (2009) were unusual in collecting a significant new data set, a historical database on government debt, whatever your views about their interpretation of the data.[1] Too few economists take the time to understand in detail how macroeconomic statistics are collected and adjusted, or to consider the conceptual issues, for example, in defining the production boundary delineating what we count as being in 'the economy', or making quality adjustments in measuring how much prices of goods such as consumer electronics have changed. There is no such thing as 'real GDP' out in the world; it is a constructed, not an observable, phenomenon. There are real events in the economy—how much income a certain household has to spend and the prices it pays for things—but these are the territory of microeconomic analysis of large surveys (with their own biases and uncertainties). Aggregate, macroeconomic, variables are ideas. Alan Greenspan, the former Federal Reserve Board chairman, was famous for his interest in detailed industry-level statistics because his concern for detail was so unusual. Nevertheless, for all the many genuine improvements made to macro modelling and forecasting since the GFC, macroeconomists have continued to make strong claims and engage in polemic: austerity is the right policy, or absolutely the wrong one; monetary policy needs to be run

1. Reinhart and Rogoff were influential in persuading Western governments to adopt austerity policies, focusing on the reduction of government debt levels. Their work was subsequently found to have involved an embarrassing spreadsheet error, leading critics refuting the apparent impact of a debt threshold on subsequent growth. Policy-makers had anyway arguably interpreted the idea of a threshold too mechanically.

according to MMT (modern monetary theory—Kelton 2020), or MMT is a half-baked, incoherent policy (Rogoff 2019).

Moreover, it is almost impossible to distinguish competing theories from each other on the basis of these aggregate macro statistics. It seems clear to me that more arguments about different theories and econometric manipulations of existing data will not resolve such issues. Macroeconomics is inherently difficult, and I do not believe it can progress further without taking account of innovation, of institutional structures in key markets such as finance, construction, and energy, of quality changes in important goods markets such as consumer electronics and housing, of regional differences, of artefacts of aggregation in the data, and so on—or in other words becoming less aggregated. Perhaps this reflects my own experience writing a macroeconomic PhD dissertation— which taught me that all industries behave completely differently over the course of a business cycle, requiring different theories, meaning the macroeconomic outcomes are the artefacts of aggregation. Or my later experience running a model forecasting the UK economy, and understanding the fudges and tweaks that all forecasters have to make to get meaningful results. Alternative approaches such as agent-based modelling, designed to deal with complexity in social science, should be explored seriously in seeking to understand the whole economy, although it does not seem to have got very far (Axtell and Epstein 1996; Farmer and Foley 2009). Standard macroeconomics has reached its limits. Ed Leamer is even more pessimistic than I am: 'Our understanding of causal effects in macroeconomics is virtually nil, and will remain so. Don't we know that?' (Leamer 2010).

This is not to despair of the project of turning economics as a whole into a more soundly-based empirical science. But we do not have nearly enough data. We do not interpret it with sufficient care. And we over-claim for our knowledge.

Nor do we use evidence to inform theorising enough, either. The scientific method is a combination of deductive and inductive reasoning, a duet between theory and data. Biology became a science through decades of careful observation and data collection, permitting inductive reasoning, which combined with deductive thinking about the biological processes involved. In economics we do not seem to have the habit of that interplay between deduction and induction needed for scientific progress. Not enough economists talk to people, visit businesses and interview managers, collect new data, run their own surveys, read history—although there are hopeful signs this is changing. Even new econometric techniques risk becoming another way of forcing a deductive approach onto reality, because of an enthusiasm for strong causal conclusions.

Policy in Wonderland

What does all this mean for the practicalities of drawing up policies and assessing policy impact? As Chapter One argued, economists in practice tend to ignore the consequences of economics being a social science, involving sentient beings who—all too often—change their behaviour in response to policy changes, or even policy debate. Of course, economists know this. While we have Goodhart's Law described earlier (that targeting a variable changes its behaviour), in the context of macroeconomics we also have the Lucas Critique (stating that historical relationships are no guide to the future when there are structural changes in the economy such as a new technology or different labour laws), but too often ignore the implications. For we imagine we can stand outside the context we are evaluating.

The habit of taking a perspective standing outside what we are evaluating also often disguises a transition from objective or 'positive' assessments to highly subjective or 'normative' conclusions. Milton Friedman, in his well-known essay on the distinction between positive and normative economics, was adamant that objective conclusions can and should be the aim. He said:

> [D]ifferences about economic policy among disinterested citizens derive predominantly from different predictions about the economic consequences of taking action—differences that in principle can be eliminated by the progress of positive economics—rather than from fundamental differences in basic values . . . a consensus on 'correct' economic policy depends much less on the progress of normative economics proper than, on the progress of a positive economics yielding conclusions that are, and deserve to be, widely accepted (Friedman 1966).

But, on the contrary, economic advice often brings in values. At the most basic level, economists can forget to include any behavioural reaction in their assessments, as noted earlier. Unfortunately, reality is like the game of croquet Alice finds herself playing in Wonderland, when the mallet turns out to be a flamingo and the ball a hedgehog, and both creatures object. Alice is the policy economist, assuming the subjects of her intervention will respond in a fixed way. They do not. They are affected by each other, and the path their decisions take over time is impossible to predict. Gregory Bateson said that in social science the game is to discover the rules of the game (Bateson 2000). They are confusingly self-referential or reflexive, but unlike researchers in some of the other social sciences many economists do not consider this characteristic.

Some examples of this kind of oversight were noted in Chapter One. One of my first insights came as a member of the UK Competition Commission's 2003 inquiry into the market for extended warranties. The market for these contracts extending the manufacturers' warranties on electrical goods (which we did find to be uncompetitive) came into existence in place of people using their domestic insurance policies to cover breakdowns. In 1997, the Treasury increased the tax on this insurance cover for domestic electrical goods to 17.5 percent, to match the rate of VAT (a sales tax) at the time. It was intended to level the playing field. However, retailers can recover much of their VAT paid back from the tax authority, so the biggest retailer of washing machines and fridges came up with the idea of (tax-free) extended warranty contracts, service contracts rather than insurance policies, implying a nice 17.5 percent profit margin. A £16 billion a year market, from which little consumer welfare derived, was born because an official assessing the tax increase had not thought that retailers might change their offer (Competition Commission 2003).

It is worth noting that similar evaluation errors can crop up in RCTs as well. It is built into them whenever the subjects are asked to give informed consent—which is generally the case thanks to academic research ethics requirements. The knowledge that you are being assessed in an experiment, even if you do not know whether or not you are in the control group or the test group, changes your behaviour and potentially biases the results. RCTs should not seek informed consent from their subjects if the experimenter is aiming to isolate a causal lever that will deliver outcomes; but this is obviously problematic. Natural field experiments of course do not suffer this bias.

Even when individual behavioural responses to a policy or intervention are taken into account, though, aggregate or social responses are inherently unpredictable. Individuals respond to each other as well as to the outsider, the policy-maker. These mutual influences are not predictable in advance. This is what it means to describe the economy as a dynamic complex system. As Paul Ormerod has been pointing out for years, we can predict in generalities but not specifics: we can talk about typical patterns, or perhaps very short-term trends, as meteorologists or seismologists do (Ormerod 1999). This again means that the economic model alone will never provide the advice the policy-maker needs; it will need to be supplemented with other kinds of evidence, and with experience and indeed with politics, which is the art of collective influence.

The tension between observing and, inevitably, participating is common to all the social sciences, but economists seem far less likely than other social scientists to pay attention to it. The economist's outsider perspective is problematic at the level of reality. It is also problematic at the level of morality. Our aim in using economics in the policy arena is to serve the public interest. We have in mind a concept of social welfare. Surely it is right to aim for the perspective of the impartial observer, to try to make an objective assessment of the welfare effects of a policy intervention. This is a constant theme of liberal theories of justice, such as John Rawls's (1971) famous 'veil of ignorance' or Adam Smith's 'impartial spectator'. At the same time, we know that economists and policy advisers are only human, responding to incentives and maximising our own utility. This is exactly why public choice theory and the New Public Management (Lapuente and Van de Walle 2020) came to emphasise the personal incentives and interests of decision-makers.

This contradictory mix of idealism and dirty realism about serving the public interest may help explain why cynicism about policy has set in, both among citizens and, indeed, among some policy-makers. In another example of economics shaping the world, there is some evidence that theories like New Public Management have to a regrettable extent undermined the ethos of public service among its providers and thus the credibility of public service with citizens; working in a policy framework determined by the theory, there is some (although mixed) evidence that public sector workers have come to behave more like the kind of self-interested agents they were theorised to be (Corduneanu, Dudau, and Kominis 2020). Earlier, I argued that to become more realistic or evidence-based, economics would have to incorporate other motivations apart from utility- or income- or profit-maximisation. Taking identity and social norms into account would perhaps have changed the advice economists gave about performance-related pay or contracting out in the public sector; or in other domains where there is unease about the market having gone 'too far'. Authors like Michael Sandel, proclaiming that the market economy has breached moral limits, have struck a chord, especially with their observation that market-based policies have changed values for the worse (Besley 2013).

There is a further tension about moving from impact assessment to social welfare assessment. Logical coherence is neutral about goals, but any assessment of impact in the world of policy has to be an assessment of the public interest with respect to certain goals. All too often in policy assessment, there is a segue from measures of economic impact regarded as objective to value judgements. This too has contributed to what many people, post-crisis, regard as market philosophy gone mad. The economist often seems to move from, say, observing that consumers in fact spend more on Dan Brown's novels rather than on those of Albert Camus (despite the recent popularity of *La Peste*), to the inference that Brown's work is inherently superior to Camus'. Yes, Dan Brown's novels do better on the popular enjoyment dimension, but worse on the dimension of literary quality.

Andrew Gelman argues that this switch from the positive to the normative, usually implicitly made, is a widespread tendency among economists; he cites an example from the Freakonomics blog, which complained that the award of the Oscar for best movie to *Argo* ignores the fact that *The Avengers* is best because it earned $200m more than the next biggest movie at the box office. Gelman notes:

1. On one hand, you have the purely descriptive perspective: economist as person-from-Mars, looking at human society objectively, the way a scientist studies cell cultures in a test tube. Consumer sovereignty is what it's all about, with a slightly offended tone that anyone could think otherwise. Who are you, smartypants, to think you know better than the average ticket-buyer? . . .

2. At the same time, we're given a moral lesson. The Avengers is the best movie because it made more money. It is 'the people who pay the bills' whose 'opinion should matter to this industry' (Gelman 2013).

I do not know how widespread such switches are, but clearly the most popular is not (always) the best, and the people whose choices define the most popular do not even think so.

To pile on the contradictions, while economists are often very uncomfortable about making explicit normative judgements of this kind, preferring to believe that our recommendations stick to the territory of positive economics, behavioural economics is inherently paternalistic. This is because of its construction that people make 'non-rational' or 'biased' decisions, which implies 'rational' is better. For instance, economics predicts that rational consumers will use APRs to compare the cost of loans, but if that were the case none of us would borrow on credit cards, never mind take out payday loans. This means behavioural economics may prove more effective in policies ranging from financial and consumer regulation to social policy. Yet the idea of 'choice architecture' to 'nudge' people towards decisions that are better for them—albeit on their own criteria—inevitably turns economists into paternalists, or even the policy wonk equivalents of Vance Packard's *Hidden Persuaders* (1957) showing how marketers and advertisers could manipulate consumers. It implies that economic analysts know what people's 'true' preferences would be, if only they were not vulnerable to behavioural 'biases' (Sugden 2020).

I have described three ambiguities or contradictions about our perspective as economists—are we inside the model or outside? Impartial observer or self-interested agent? Does the paternalistic economist know best, or is the consumer king?

The ambiguities matter because economists present themselves as technocratic experts in the domain of public policy, the toilers after truth discovering 'what works'. Exciting new techniques like RCTs, recognized in the 2019 Nobel Prize in economics, encourage this self-perception of the economist as objective scientist, now literally experimenting on society. Abhijit Banerjee and Esther Duflo wrote in their post-Nobel book *Good Economics for Hard Times* (2019) (writing about immigration policy, pretty contentious): 'This underscores the urgent need to set ideology aside and advocate for things most economists agree on, based on the recent research.' Here again is a claim to the possibility of impartiality.

However, the successful project of empirical microeconomics is putting economics ever more firmly into the political arena, the arena of normative choices.

For example, RCTs or econometric evaluations will sometimes produce conclusions that run against politically acceptable ideas. One study by University of Chicago researchers into what incentives produced the largest impact on test scores for Chicago schoolchildren found that by a long way the biggest effect came from paying teachers *in advance* a large bonus conditional on their pupils' results; the power of loss aversion meant these teachers were determined to achieve the outcomes so they would be able to keep the money (Fryer et al. 2012). How would advance bonuses in the public sector play politically? This is, of course, a rhetorical question. The findings of RCTs may well conflict with political or cultural beliefs about the right course of action. Perhaps economic efficiency is not the societal goal in all contexts, so other people's idea of a good outcome might be different from even the most balanced, open-minded economist.

In the current conjuncture, in the post-GFC, deglobalisation, mid-pandemic, western economies, economists claiming to be technocrats are very definitely taking political positions. As the prominent UK politician Michael Gove notoriously expressed the populist position in the 2016 Brexit referendum campaign, 'People have had enough of experts.' Or at least experts whose conclusions they disagree with. Some people even distrust medical expertise, on issues like vaccines or coronavirus treatments, even though their distrust could be lethal. What hope for the impartial, scientific economist? Expertise has inevitably become political when populism is widespread (Moore 2017).

Conclusions

I began by saying that economists make the same mistake as Camus' Outsider: it is not possible to stand apart, disengaged from the society we are studying. The outsider perspective has become unsustainable in polarised societies. In short, political economy is back. It is certainly back in a no-growth or recessionary economy with no rising tide to make distributional shifts acceptable. And it is back because the genuine advances in economics in the past couple of decades, in empirical microeconomic research, will bring more examples of conflicts between 'what works' assessed according to the efficiency criterion of the 'objective' economist and what people believe or want even if it is not rational, or not even reasonable.

Intermission

The lecture on which Chapter Two draws angered at least one member of my audience, a well-known UK macroeconomist. The next day he sent me an email that began, 'I thought your talk last night was shabby and ungracious, to say the least. It hardly helps to slag off half the profession, particularly in convoluted jargon.' And continued by saying he for one had forecast the GFC: 'I wrote in September, 2004 . . . the first statement of the savings-glut idea, which made it easy to see the inevitability of a financial crisis. Several other economists correctly forecast the crisis arising from US household borrowing. I suggest you do your research by reading this material before next opining on macro-economics.'

Indeed, some economists did foresee a crisis, though it is fair to say the weight of professional opinion prior to 2008 did not, for those who could claim such foresight certainly made sure the world knew afterwards. I was taken aback by the strength of my correspondent's reaction, but not enough to change my mind. Macroeconomics is genuinely hard, and despite all the post-GFC improvements in models—for example, by adding financial 'frictions', heterogeneity (that is, differences between firms or types of individuals), and being more explicit about uncertainty—I do not find the prevailing strategy is persuasive when it comes to modelling the whole economy and forecasting its future.

Why so? For two main reasons, outlined above. One is that there is too little macroeconomic data. Since the GFC my own research has focused on economic statistics (particularly how we measure digital activities), so I have thought about the data far more than ever before. Figures for the variables in macroeconomic models such as GDP, or inflation and unemployment, change relatively little from quarter to quarter and are often strongly correlated with each other. Even if you accept 'inflation' as a uniquely definable indicator (and it is not), there are large margins of error in its measurement. Identifying cause and effect, or any stable relationships between variables in this context is—I believe—impossible. Information from outside the model itself needs to be brought to bear, such as historical narrative, or a strongly held prior theory based on other kinds of evidence and methods.

The second reason is that it is not obvious what the right level of aggregation ought to be, or how to move from the behaviour of an individual or firm—which is what economic theory addresses—to any aggregation of them. Countries have national macroeconomic statistics for political reasons: national governments operate national policies. But the political boundaries will hardly ever correspond to natural economic boundaries. City regions, or cross-border supply chains, might be the right level of analysis. And the collective, social outcomes may very well not add up to the aggregated ones anyway. The experience of pandemic and lockdown illustrates the vast uncertainties very well: there was much debate mid-2020 about the likely 'shape' of the recovery (V, U, W, L, or even a square root symbol √) given the recognition that whether people returned to spending would depend on—whether people returned to spending. Confidence would determine the path.

I have no doubt many macroeconomists will disagree with me, perhaps as strongly as my correspondent quoted above— although when I ran into him at an event some years later, he chatted to me cheerfully as if nothing had happened. Had he forgotten sending me the email? Or just forgiven me?

Still, as time moved on from the GFC the shortcomings of macro were less at the front of my mind, and my own work on the digital economy preoccupied me more. I also changed careers. In 2014 I switched from policy and consulting to the academic world, becoming a Professor of Economics at the University of Manchester in 2014. There, I introduced a course on public policy economics—it later became the basis of my 2020 book, *Markets, State and People*. For the first time in many years I started to mull over what economists refer to as 'social welfare': how well off is society as a whole? As this next chapter describes, I was not the only economist to have not thought much about this question; few had done so for some decades. Chapter Three picks up on the points above about positive and normative economics building on a seminar presentation at All Souls College, Oxford in spring 2017 and a lecture at the September 2017 conference of the International Network for Economic Method; this was later turned into an academic article (Coyle 2019a). It expands on some of the themes of Chapters One and Two, particularly about rational choice and *homo economicus*, and was also informed by the two years or so I spent as a Fellow (unpaid) of AI company DeepMind's Ethics and Society group.

So the main question posed in this chapter is how should we assess whether our expert policy advice is making things better, or not, and particularly when digital transformation is changing the character of the economy so much.

3

Homo Economicus, AIs, Rats and Humans

Rationality in the Wild

Take three kinds of experiment.

The artificial intelligence (AI) company DeepMind set its AI agents—decision-making rules on a computer—competing for scarce resources in an apple-picking game (Leibo et al. 2017a,b). The game, 'Gathering', aimed to explore whether the agents would co-operate to gather apples, or whether they would free ride, that is consume the apples other agents had already gathered. These AIs used deep reinforcement learning, meaning the algorithmic agent, 'Must learn to maximize its cumulative long-term reward through trial-and-error interactions with its environment.' In other words, the computer agent teaches itself from certain sensory inputs—such as the location of pixels on screen in a game—and its own experience of whether what happens next adds to its own score. The agents were designed to make decisions like *homo economicus*, rational actors in a classic economic model of constrained optimization, in other words maximising their score subject to the availability of apples, interacting with each other over time as the game played out. Each formed part of the environment to which it had to respond. All was harmony when apples were plentiful. But when they became scarcer, the AIs became more aggressive, ultimately attacking each other. It was war for apples. The greater the competition for resources, the more aggressive the AIs.

You might conclude that this is what is bound to happen when the agents are programmed to act in their calculated self-interest, like the construct of *homo economicus* in neoclassical economics. Economists are habituated to this idea as a sort of initial benchmark for analysis, but many critics find this assumption both unrealistic and immoral. It is obviously right as a matter of fact to say that humans often demonstrate altruism or concern for others. Bowles (2004) argues that any account of economic decision making must incorporate people using rules of thumb, rather than rational calculation if it is to be minimally valid empirically. The expanding behavioural economics and psychology literature, largely based on experiments of another kind, supports the case for a broader view of how humans take decisions. In human reality, it is not a war of all against all in the economy, unlike the AI game. And in fact alternative assumptions to *homo economicus* have come to be widely used in applied economics, even though it remains the most common starting point (Pesendorfer 2006).

Outside both the artificial world of the computer and the offline world of humans, a third category of experiments has looked at the behaviour of many biological creatures in conditions of resource scarcity. Sometimes these experimental subjects, such as rats or pigeons, demonstrate emotional reactions, such as sharing with a friend, or punishing cheats even at a cost to themselves. But entities ranging from bacteria and fungi to capuchin monkeys also often seem to act like self-interested calculators, acting just like the agents of economic models or AI games. For example, they are willing to write off sunk costs, calculate probabilities correctly, and seem to have in mind consistent exchange rates of grapes for cucumbers. These are all choices that would be predicted by economic models of constrained optimisation (De Waal 2006; Hammerstein and Noë 2016; Herbranson and Schroeder 2010; Hurley and Nudds 2006). The kind of trade that takes place in these 'biological markets' appears to be reasonably consistent with the models of mainstream economics.

What are we to make of these three types of experimental result? Surely not that rats are more rational than us and that compared to AIs we are nice but dim. The contrasts cannot be about cognitive capacity, as fungi and bacteria have no neurons. This is not a question about similarities or differences in the 'deep plumbing' of the minds of different kinds of creature (or algorithms). The similarities and differences in behaviour must be linked to the outside world, not the inner, to the contexts within which evolutionary processes of specialisation and exchange by individual entities, subject to resource constraints, operate.

Individual human choices have a social as well as an environmental context. We make decisions amid a greater social complexity than many other biological creatures, or AI agents. And as Leibo et al. (2017a,b) conclude: 'The complexity of learning how to implement effective cooperation and defection policies may not be equal. One or the other might be significantly easier to learn.' Indeed. Co-operation, it turns out, requires a lot of computational resource; self-interested maximisation is easy by comparison. Scarce resources make co-operation more costly. Context is everything.

This conclusion is not unknown in economics. Long ago Becker (1962) showed that market outcomes looking as though they are the outcome of rational choice subject to constraints sometimes come about even when individual choices are wholly 'irrational', either random or unchanging. The market outcome is the result of context, with no need to assume anything about individual psychology or preferences. More broadly, economists have a renewed interest in context, at least in the shape of history and geography. Much interesting research is happening on the borders with a range of disciplines, not just psychology and cognitive science, but also history, geography, information theory, evolutionary biology, complexity science, and political economy. Yet the immense interest in behavioural economics may turn out to be a red herring if we take seriously the insight from both biological markets theory and information theory, that context rather than cognition is what matters. We should be trying to figure out the relevant contexts that shape decisions instead.

There is still a lot we have to learn about human decision making in economics.

The Separation Protocol: Is and Ought

The experimental results are factual or empirical questions: how to describe and model observed choices. They are questions of 'is', rather than 'ought'. What about the ethics of the *homo economicus* assumption? Some critics would argue that assuming calculating self-interested behaviour encourages people to act in unethical ways. It gives a justification for such behaviour, or a social signal that it is acceptable. The last chapter noted the possible loss of intrinsic public service motivation due to the adoption of New Public Management policies inspired by public choice theory. Bowles (2016) and Sandel (2012) offer examples of policies based on the assumption of self-interest inducing people to behave more selfishly than they otherwise would. A well-known example is the story of the nursery that started fining parents for picking up their children late—the fines simply made people think they were paying for extra care and did not deter lateness.

In contrast to the lively interest in the psychology of decision making demonstrated by the popularity of behavioural economics, this line of criticism has drawn little response from economists. The reason is that so many of us have little professional interest in ethical questions: we think the 'is' and the 'ought' are separate questions, and economics is about the 'is'. Philosophers can deal with the rest.

Yet there is a whole branch of economics that is concerned with ethical questions. Although welfare economics—the study of the benefit to society of economic outcomes or choices— necessarily underpins policy evaluation, and is widely used in practical contexts (such as cost-benefit analysis or competition assessments), economists have paid little attention to it in recent times. Indeed, economics has insisted for more than eighty years on a strict separation between 'is' and 'ought', between 'positive' and 'normative'. Pigou (1908) represented an older tradition, writing: 'Ethics and economics are mutually dependent.' Adam Smith made the same link. While realistic about human nature, he observed that everyone appreciates that 'his own interest is connected with the prosperity of society' (Smith 2000 [1759]; see also Rothschild 2001). But in a departure from this tradition, the positivist movement represented in economics by Lionel Robbins led the discipline to rule out inter-personal welfare comparisons. If we cannot compare losses and gains experienced by different people, it is impossible to make substantive comments about the social welfare implications of any policy choice.

In a famous essay, 'The Nature and Significance of Economic Science', Robbins (1932) claimed that economics and ethics were on 'different planes': 'Economics is neutral as between ends. Economics cannot pronounce on the validity of ultimate judgments of value.' Since then, economics has adhered to the idea that its role is to pronounce on means and not on ends—there is a strict separation protocol. Value judgements are to be left to others, such as elected politicians. In another well-known essay, Milton Friedman (1953, 146) was even more explicit:

> Positive economics is in principle independent of any particular ethical position or normative judgments. . . . Its task is to provide a system of generalizations that can be used to make correct predictions about the consequences of any change in circumstances. Its performance is to be judged by the precision, scope, and conformity with experience of the predictions it yields. In short, positive economics is, or can be, an 'objective' science, in precisely the same sense as any of the physical sciences.

Many economists continue to see their discipline as largely contributing 'positive' insights, even if agreeing that many policy choices involve value judgements. There is something admirable about trying to keep personal ethics out of expert advice. We surely want our experts to try to be as objective and impartial as possible. And in the flourishing domain of applied microeconomics, economists are indeed able to build a growing evidence base for policy choices.

However, the separation protocol calls into question how to assess the results—the social welfare gain or loss—in many practical applications of economics to policy choices (Hausman and McPherson 2006). The protocol is generally expressed as what is known the Pareto criterion: a policy can only be said to increase social welfare if it makes at least one person better off, and no one worse off. This is so obviously extraordinarily restrictive that economists have often argued (following Hicks [1939] and Kaldor [1939]) that a policy is welfare improving if the winners can (at least in theory) compensate the losers. This is sometimes called the potential Pareto improvement criterion. However, Scitovszky (1941) not long after, and subsequent authors (Baumol 1952; Roberts 1980), have demonstrated that depending on whose perspective you take—the winners' or the losers'—both the policy and its reversal can be beneficial on the Pareto criterion. As Baumol put it, the Hicks-Kaldor compensation suggestion:

> [H]as not eliminated the problem of interpersonal comparison of utility. It has only subjected utility to the measuring rod of money, a measuring rod which bends and stretches and ultimately falls to pieces in our hands (Baumol 1952, 89).

Economics has hamstrung its ability to evaluate social welfare by deeming situations where there are winners and losers—which is almost all policy contexts—to be out of scope.

Of course, aggregating individual gains and losses to calculate aggregate outcomes for society is not an easy task. Welfare economists have long noted that *any* aggregation involves an implicit value judgement about the distribution of resources (Graaff 1957): how much do we weight people at different parts of the income distribution when we aggregate? Everybody equal? More weight on improvements for the worst-off? In principle, the concept of a social welfare function (SWF) (Bergson 1938; Samuelson 1983) explicitly reintroduced ethical judgements about distribution. The policy-maker can specify an objective function—say equal outcomes, or improving things the most for the worst-off person (the maximin criterion)—and aggregate individual utilities with appropriate weights. However, in his famous (Im)possibility Theorem, Kenneth Arrow (1950) established that there is no way of consistently adding up individual utilities to calculate social welfare that will satisfy the Pareto criterion, and a few other seemingly reasonable assumptions. Arrow's theorem is really a formal statement of the obvious truth that there are unavoidable conflicts of interest or dilemmas in society. The 'impossibility' is the result of a clash between trying to make a value judgement in terms of an SWF while excluding the possibility of interpersonal welfare comparisons. In life, the scope for Pareto improvements is small indeed.

Economics students are rarely exposed to these dilemmas. Arrow is mentioned reverentially, only to then sit quietly on his pedestal. Young economists are taught that, under certain assumptions, the competitive market equilibrium is Pareto efficient; and that given any initial allocation of resources, a Pareto efficient outcome can be reached through market exchange. These are known as the first and second welfare theorems. The necessary assumptions include, for instance, rational, self-interested choice, full information, fixed preferences, and an absence of externalities (such as pollution) or public goods (such as defence of the realm of clean air). They form an interesting and useful framework for analysing what kinds of policies or government interventions in the 'free market' might be needed, but they are certainly invalid. Perhaps the most significant divergence between assumptions and reality is the gap between the individual and social. For example, in an industry with increasing returns to scale, each individual firm's production decision will affect all the others in the industry. Or, my preferences for different goods I might purchase are certainly not fixed, or Apple would never have bothered inventing the iPhone, or advertising it.

Despite their failure to account for the social aspects of the economy, the welfare theorems have made the idea of competitive markets a powerful benchmark. It was cemented into place in policy choices by the co-evolution of events, political developments and economic ideas in the 1970s and '80s. Margaret Thatcher and Ronald Reagan embedded in their philosophies of government a free market version of economics. The macroeconomic failures of the 1970s and the collapse of the centrally planned economies in 1989 seemed to validate this shift in public policy. Academic economics in turn took it further, embracing rational expectations, public choice, and real business cycle theory, as described earlier.

The presumption in much policy analysis then became that governments should only be intervening to fix specific, identified market failures. Indeed, 'government failure' was invoked in the public choice literature as at least an equally significant pitfall for the policy-maker (Le Grand 1991). Yet, as Baumol (1952, 165) noted, the conclusion that the market knows best derives entirely from assumptions of the welfare theorems, the assumptions ruling out interdependence between individuals. The reasoning is entirely circular. If you assume individuals behave independently, independent behaviour gives the best outcomes. If you assume otherwise, analysing what is best for society as a whole becomes a far more difficult task.

Yet the separation protocol remains powerful. Economists in general see the task of the economist interested in public policy or social outcomes as technical: look at the data, identify the relevant market failures, and the appropriate correctives. Value judgements can be left to philosophers or politicians. This is fine up to a point. Given a preferred outcome, inevitably based on ethical criteria, economics does provide theoretical and empirical tools to analyse how it might be attained. The subject has a tradition from Smith (2000 [1759]) to Sen (2009) of explicitly adopting the perspective of the 'impartial spectator', taking into account other people's perspectives, in public reasoning. The majority of economists are therefore comfortable with their practice of attempting to separate value judgements, including their own, from an analysis of what is—and indeed most attempt to observe that separation honourably.

Implications for Economic Policy

Nevertheless economics is inextricably concerned with normative issues, such as whether to build a new rail line through green fields (cost-benefit analysis), or regulate the safety standards of companies' products (regulatory policy), or prevent a private transaction when one company wants to acquire another (competition policy). Economists have their own values and views, too. The separation protocol severely hampers the economic analysis of public policy questions where the underlying issue is precisely how to organise the collective use and allocation of resources.

One instance is the use of normative values in a supposedly positive way is cost-benefit analysis (CBA), a widely used tool in government. CBA tries to put all the costs and benefits of an intervention into monetary terms, preferably calculated using a competitive market price, although in practice often using a range of methods for assigning dollar or pound values. In arguing for the use of market prices, Harberger (1971) did observe that this ruled out certain dimensions people might value:

> These elements—which surely include the income-distributional and national-defense aspects of any project or program, and probably its natural-beauty aspects as

well—may be exceedingly important, perhaps even the dominant factors governing any policy decision, but they are not a part of that package of expertise that distinguishes the professional economist from the rest of humanity.

So here too is an appeal to the separation protocol. As the practice of CBA has developed, there have been efforts to take into account 'wider impacts' of policies, including environmental externalities, for example. Successive revisions of the UK Treasury's Green Book have increasingly emphasised non-market or social aspects of the calculation, from impacts on the environment to wider policy ambitions. A current example would be investing in what are described as 'left behind' regions even if the economic return might be higher—the cost-benefit assessment more positive—if the money were invested in a richer area.

CBA has been criticised in particular by environmentalists for trying to put a monetary figure on intrinsic value, on the inherently priceless (Kelman 1981). Economists have responded by making the technique more sophisticated (Drèze and Stern 1987; Dietz and Hepburn 2013). Yet its use nevertheless makes implicit rather than explicit the normative judgements in any policy decision by its use of the money metric as the common yardstick. The distribution of benefits and costs is not addressed—this is left to political decision-makers. Above all, the method assumes there is no difference between the sum of the values of costs or benefits to an individual and the social costs and benefits. Interaction and social influence are assumed away.

Many other areas of applied economics also involve a welfare assessment, yet one hamstrung by using the Pareto criterion—we have as a profession tied our hands by adopting a measure of social well-being that is indifferent to the distribution of resources. If many poor people become better off but one rich person worse off as a result of a policy, the intervention fails on the formal Pareto welfare standard we use in economics. This is so obviously undesirable that in practice policy advice over-rides the formal apparatus of welfare analysis with common sense. But we are left with a muddle. How do we decide whether a policy is a good idea or not?

The Economy's Challenge to Economics

The vacuum in welfare economics needs to be filled because of the way the economy is changing. Technology has always been social. Even an old technology such as electricity took half a century to manifest itself in higher productivity because of the need to make many complementary investments and to rearrange the organisation of work and home (David 1990). Many countries still fail to deliver a consistent electricity supply when the political and social conditions for use of the technologies involved go awry.

Recent technological innovation has increased the extent and significance of social spillovers, for example, in the form of network effects in digital markets, economics of scale, externalities in the accumulation and use of data, or agglomeration effects in economic geography. There are more market failures as a result, when private and collective interests diverge. Complex goods and services at the technological frontier in digital, genetic technology, or materials technology, involve large-scale co-operative activities, extensive communication and knowledge, and major investments in tangible and intangible infrastructure. New goods and services are often non-rival—they can be used by more than one person at a time without being depleted—and so meet the classic definition of a public good. Public goods often require public provision because they need up-front financing, but once paid for there is no additional (marginal) cost to their use so extracting payment for use may be practically difficult and will be economically inefficient.

Increasing returns to scale, externalities, and non-rival goods are pervasive in modern knowledge economies. When there is rapid technical change and rapid diffusion of new goods and services, as now, fixed preferences are even less likely to exist than in stable times when it is simply fashion or social influence or learning that changes individual preferences. Government co-ordination in terms of public-good research, technical standards, skills and so on is essential for markets to come into existence. The 'state vs. markets' dichotomy of political debate for the past generation is not a valid empirical approach to modern economies. Although there never was a market without the state (or vice versa), their mutual interdependence has increased greatly with the levels of economic complexity. The circumstances in which markets fail are exactly the circumstances in which governments fail too, because they are exactly the circumstances when private and collective interests diverge the most.

Today's digital economy is increasing the gap between the assumption of individual separability in the theorems underpinning welfare economics and the inter-dependence of individuals in actual economies. Atkinson (2001, 193) noted that students had stopped studying welfare economics by the 1960s, even though economics was increasingly full of value statements: "[D]espite the prevalence of welfare statements in modern economics, we are no longer subjecting them to critical analysis." Angus Deaton echoed this in a recent conversation with Amartya Sen (Sen, Deaton, and Besley 2020), arguing there has been no progress in welfare economics since at least the 1970s, when some classic texts (Little 1950; Graaff

1971; Sen 2017 [1970]) underlined the problem: 'If you look at where we are now, most economic departments—including top departments—have no teaching of welfare economics. That subject has just completely vanished' (Sen, Deaton, and Besley 2020, 16). Atkinson argued that economists must consider explicitly the moral consequences of their models. The economic analysis of public policy choices ultimately is not and cannot be technocratic. As individual and collective interests will often diverge, conflicts of interest and the comparison of economic welfare outcomes for different people or groups is inevitable. The Pareto criterion is of no practical use.

Developments in mainstream economics in the past decade or two may signal the profession's increasing awareness of such issues. Institutional economics is one example. Institutions by definition involve more than one individual, and are located in place and time. Governments, public bodies, universities, firms, co-ops, charities, temples, unions, families are recognised as means of reaching collective decisions about the use and allocation of resources. Institutions are shaped by asymmetric information and transactions costs—which are standard features in modern economic models—and also by social preference formation, which is not (Bowles 2004).

Interdependence is also by definition recognised in game theory, the analysis of decision-makers interacting with each other strategically, which has wide influence in economics. The area of market design is similarly inherently concerned with interdependent decisions. In the context of digital markets and financial markets, network theory is widely used, where the existence and identity of other individuals is core. Environmental economics focuses on externalities, as do studies of digital markets such as online platforms. Modern growth theory has growth depend on knowledge spillovers, in other words people learning from each other. There is a growing interest in economic applications of the science of complexity (Colander and Kupers 2014) and in evolutionary theory (Lo 2017).

More specifically relevant to welfare economics, the capabilities approach to welfare has gained policy traction, both in the context of development economics (Dasgupta 2007; Sen 2017; 1970) and in the wider debate about how to assess economic progress (Fitoussi, Sen, and Stiglitz 2009). There has been a recent surge of interest in the worlds of policy-making and campaigning, including in official bodies such as the European Commission and the Organisation for Economic Co-operation and Development (OECD), in measures that go 'beyond GDP', or in other words beyond market outcomes. Yet the technocratic instinct and the legacy of free market politics since the 1980s leave much economic policy analysis stranded in a narrower approach than is reflected in this recent thinking. Economic policy-makers who were students in earlier decades have firmly internalised the free market framing. This has been sustained because researchers have given too little thought to the welfare economics framework, which inevitably shapes the application of their findings. Although economic research has changed substantially over recent decades, increasingly incorporating interdependence rather than individualism, welfare economics has not kept up. Unless economists revisit the foundations of welfare economics—the questions of distribution and outcomes for society as a whole—our ability to speak to today's policy questions will be limited. The experiments with which this chapter began highlighted the relevance of context if we want to understand the 'is' of economic decisions; the time has come to abandon the separation protocol and think properly about the way context also affects the 'ought', and what kind of society we want to live in.

Intermission

What Chapter Three did not explicitly discuss was the changing political environment. In 2016, the 'Leave' campaigners won the UK's Brexit referendum, Donald Trump had won the US presidential election, and across the West populist parties were gaining a significant share of votes even where they lost the election. Political shifts of this kind never have a single cause, but economic disadvantage was certainly involved: studies of different votes have mapped the correlation between populist vote shares and places 'left behind' (the term in vogue) by economically-thriving big urban centres. The chickens dating back to deindustrialisation in the 1980s were coming home to roost. Although the big increases in income and wealth inequality had occurred during the 1980s, policy attention focused on this far more after the headline-grabbing Occupy movements, the success of Thomas Piketty's *Capital* (2014), and the increased awareness of the social costs of being left behind, so authoritatively documented by Anne Case and Angus Deaton in *Deaths of Despair* (2020). For many people, life had not been getting better, whatever the macroeconomic statistics said.

Inequality is a political as well as an economic phenomenon. Different OECD economies facing similar trends—new disruptive technologies, ageing populations, and globalisation of supply chains affecting trade and employment—experienced differing degrees of inequality. Their labour laws, the role of unions, social partnerships, tax policy, and other institutional features all differed depending on history and contemporary politics.

However, the economic shifts have driven similar outcomes everywhere. Regions already part of the rust belt have become even more disadvantaged because new, knowledge-based technologies require certain kinds of skills that come with a long formal education (known in economics jargon as skill-biased technical change) and also significant exchange of informal know-how (tacit, rather than codified, knowledge in the jargon). These features have led to a geographical sorting between different kinds of people. The highly-educated knowledge workers have increasingly congregated in specific large urban centres such as San Francisco and Silicon Valley, or capitals like Berlin, London, and Paris. The unevenness of economic geography has been evident since Alfred Marshall (2013) first identified what are known as 'agglomeration economies' in 1890, in other words the economic benefits of jobs and production clustering close together. It is after all what explained the rise of the great Victorian cities during the Industrial Revolution. Digital technology and the general shift in economic growth toward knowledge-based or 'weightless' activity (Coyle 1997) reinforced agglomeration economies and so widened the geographical dimension of the inequality (Autor 2019; Moretti 2012). The pandemic will certainly halt or even reverse this trend, but for how long we do not know.

What's more, the digital sector itself has created extraordinary wealth concentrated in very few hands. Some commentators

have drawn apt comparisons between the 2020s and the Gilded
Age of the 1920s, for such are the contrasts. San Francisco sym-
bolises the chasm between rich and poor: a large homeless population in desperate state down the road from millionaires and
billionaires, who watch the destitute and addicted through the
windows of their Uber or the executive shuttle to Menlo Park or
Mountain View (Chan 2017; Solnit 2014). There is now an active
policy debate about tackling tech wealth and power, much of it
focused on the dominance of digital markets by a small number
of giant companies. The biggest—Alphabet (Google), Amazon,
Apple, Facebook, Microsoft—became even more successful as
the pandemic moved so much more activity online.

The way digital is reshaping our economic and social lives
has been my focus since the 1990s. In fact, it was an experience
as a new reporter on *The Independent* newspaper in 1994 that
triggered a lasting interest. The technology stock market bubble
had not yet happened, so nobody more senior on the business
desk was interested in covering the flotation through a stock
market IPO of a small technology company from Cambridge
called Unipalm. It was the UK's first commercial internet service provider. I wasn't sure what that was, but dutifully went
along to the hotel suite the company's PR firm had rented for the
roadshow demonstration to investors and financial journalists.
The highlight of the presentation was a webcam showing traffic
moving across the Golden Gate Bridge in San Francisco—live,
under our eyes. If this sounds unexciting now, remember that
this was the same era when a webcam on a Cambridge University coffee pot, connected to the new World Wide Web, became
a popular phenomenon.[1] Anyway, I was impressed; something

---

1. 'Trojan Room Coffee Pot', Wikipedia, https://en.wikipedia.org/wiki/Trojan
_Room_coffee_pot.

instantly convinced me this would be a big thing—although not impressed enough to actually invest any money in tech stocks. Instead, I wrote a book about it.

Since then, through my career changes over twenty-odd years, digital has been a focus of my work, writing about it, working on technology economics as a consultant, analysing the markets as a regulator, and now researching it. Chapter Four, which uses some material from my 2018 inaugural lecture at the University of Cambridge,[2] continues the discussion from the previous chapter about the way digitalisation forces a rethink of welfare economics, or how we know whether society is getting better off. This encompasses a discussion about how we measure progress, picking up from Chapter Three's discussion of social welfare and normative considerations, and the wedge between GDP and social welfare created by digital phenomena. The next chapter also introduces a new question: does the technology also force a rethink about the effectiveness of economic policies? What is the relationship between government and market in the digital world?

2. 'Cogs and Monsters', Bennett Institute for Public Policy, Cambridge University, https://www.bennettinstitute.cam.ac.uk/publications/cogs-and-monsters/.

4

Cogs and Monsters

For anybody interested in public policy there is a fundamental question, all too rarely explicitly addressed: what does it mean for policy to make things better? What is the outcome the policy is supposed to achieve, and what would make any particular outcome better than another? This can be answered in relatively narrow terms: competition policy should increase or maintain competition; monetary policy should achieve stable inflation; and so on. But that just puts the question at one remove by assuming these narrow goals are the appropriate ones. How do these make society as a whole better off, and how can we tell?

In economics—always so central to public policy debates—machine metaphors are deeply embedded in our language and thinking (Lakoff and Johnson 1980). In the twentieth century this was taken literally enough that the Phillips Machine, of which there are a few left (Figure 2), was taken to represent the economy as a whole, literally mechanical relationships of pipes and cogs. How naïve we were to think this was an adequate

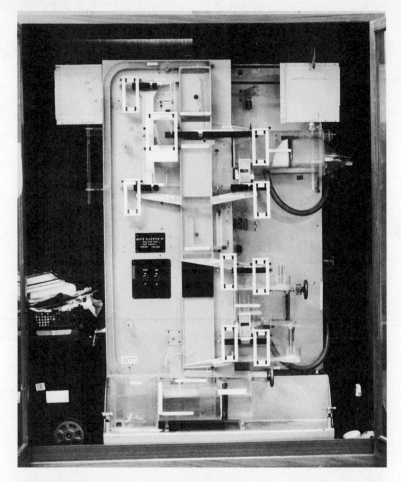

FIGURE 2. The Phillips Machine, Author's photo, Meade Room, Faculty of Economics, Cambridge

model of the economy. We know better now, with (metaphorical) models incorporating uncertainty, frictions, expectations, shocks, behavioural biases. Yet the machine metaphor is still deeply embedded in economic policy. We speak of policy levers, of linkages, of cause and effect. When asked to reflect on their discipline, economists often reach for comparisons with engineers (Roth 2002) or plumbers (Duflo 2017).

Needless to say, the world is not mechanical, and we are not the cogs in a machine assumed in the models. The continuing economic, social, and political transformations driven by technological change are, paradoxically, making our increasingly machine-run world ever less mechanistic and predictable. As in mediaeval maps, there are monsters in the unknown territories beyond the boundaries of current knowledge. The new monsters are symbolised by the nightmare robot creations of Boston Dynamics.[1]

Digital transformation of everyday life, of business and consumption, of social relations and politics, raises two questions. One is an old question requiring new answers: what kind of society do we want, and how do we measure progress towards it? The second is what makes policies effective in delivering progress in this non-linear, complex world, that is not amenable to simple causal explanations?

What Counts as Progress in a Digital World?

The story starts with digital technology. Its consequences are certainly not deterministic, but as a 'general purpose technology' used widely across the economy, it sparks innovation, changes behaviour, and forces reactions and significant adjustments in the economy and society. The growing use of artificial intelligence (AI) or machine learning (ML) systems seems likely to accelerate this. The pervasive effects of the new

1. 'Parkour Atlas', Boston Dynamics, YouTube, https://www.youtube.com/watch?v=LikxFZZO2sk; 'UpTown Spot', Boston Dynamics, YouTube, https://www.youtube.com/watch?v=kHBcVlqpvZ8, accessed 18 October 2018.

technologies on economic and social life are driving a reassess-
ment of the current framework for classifying and measuring
the economy, especially the shorthand indicator of economic
progress, GDP. The evidence of huge technologically-driven
change is everywhere in daily life, and almost nowhere in the
standard economic statistics. Once GDP growth is questioned
as a measure of progress for any single reason, it also raises
other reasons to doubt its usefulness—it fails to reflect income
distribution, omits valuable unpaid work, ignores the environment. Its inadequacies become a symbol of the failure of
technocratic economists to deliver improvements in life for
too many citizens. The standard policy success metrics have
rendered some important phenomena invisible for too long.
Expertise is a claim to authority over the lives of others, so
if it fails to deliver it is not surprising that people challenge
the constraints it imposes on them, by voting for anti-elitists,
for example.

The kind of structural changes the technology brings about
distorts the statistical lens through which we observe progress.
A new framework for measuring progress is needed. Reflecting
on measurement in the context of major economic and societal change reinforces an old but often forgotten lesson: while
statistics reflect some underlying features of reality, they are
never value free (Porter 1995; Desrosières 2002). Nor indeed
is economists' influence in modern government despite the
claim to value-free technical know-how, as Chapter Three
discussed.

When I was a teenager in the 1970s, there was no internet
or web, no mobile telephony, no personal computers or tab-
lets or smartphones, and none of the services such as search,
streaming music or movies, email, text messaging. Phones were

tethered to the wall, usually in a cold hall (as central heating was far from universal), and the line was often shared with a neighbour. Vinyl was still on its first run although cassette tapes were now available as an alternative. Banking meant going to the high street and queuing. Cars used toxic leaded petrol, burned less efficiently, had no radios or electric windows, none of today's safety systems, still less built-in GPS and air conditioning. MRI scanners had not been invented, nor today's drugs for cancer; cataract and varicose vein surgery were not simple outpatient procedures. As well as obviously significant innovations like the internet or medical or pharmaceutical advances, there have been a multitude of incremental improvements in everyday life: outdoor gear made from fabrics that really do keep out the wind and rain, disposable contact lenses, tights that do not immediately ladder, the ability to watch TV programmes when you want, energy-efficient light bulbs. The combination in 2008 of the spread of smartphones, 3G mobile networks and algorithms embedding market design was particularly transformative. Whole industries from taxis to accommodation to retail have been 'disrupted' ever since.

Equally pervasive and significant innovations have occurred in the equipment used by businesses and the ways they operate, including the automation of production processes and the extension of the just-in-time production system across whole supply chains. Like earlier important technologies, digital, and now AI, are reshaping the economy entirely. Without the post-1980s development in information and communication technologies, there would have been far less economic globalisation in multinational operations, no reorganisation of business in the shape of outsourcing and 'delayering' or reducing the number of middle managers, no business model innovations such as digital platforms, no on-demand services and e-commerce, no social media.

The economy of mass production reached its apogee by the 1960s, and the turning point became evident with the economic crises of the 1970s. By the mid-1980s Paul Romer had started publishing his work on the role of knowledge in economic growth (for which he was later awarded the Nobel memorial prize), underlining the way it changes economic phenomena (Romer 1986a, b). In the knowledge economy, growth is like a snowball gathering ever-greater mass as it rolls downhill. Increasing returns to scale are pervasive in leading sectors such as information technology or biotechnology. Small changes in policy or other decisions lead to very large difference in outcomes. There are tipping points as things that start small, like a digital platform, suddenly become very big indeed. There is also path dependency or lock-in—it is almost impossible to switch trajectories once the direction of change has been established, particularly when it comes to things like embedding technical standards or building a mass customer base.

More goods and services, intangible and based on ideas, are non-rival—software, for instance, can be copied more or less for free for many users without limiting the first user. Similarly with data, which is not depleted by repeated use. This makes data formally a public good, although of course people can be excluded from using it, either by technology such as encryption or by law: intellectual property law including patents and copyrights is widely deployed to constrain the wide use of intangible goods.[2]

In general, more goods involve externalities or complementarities making them more useful or valuable when they

2. Public goods from which people can be excluded are known as club goods.

are produced and consumed collectively rather than individually. One response to the concern about big digital companies harvesting our data and using it to make money at our expense is the suggestion that the data harvesters should pay us—providing personal data is a form of labour and should be rewarded, the argument goes (Arrietta-Ibarra et al. 2018). Yet one individual's attention just isn't worth all that much. The individualistic solution leaves the social value unallocated. Digital companies extract some of this by aggregating our individual data for marketing or for sale to advertisers.

However, the confinement of data within the servers of individual companies and its portrayal as 'personal' fail to crystallise all the potential social value. For the aggregate is worth more than the individual, and different types of data joined to each other are worth more still (Coyle et al. 2020). We could potentially benefit more from the regularities machine learning could discover from combining many people's data on their food shopping habits, health status, web browsing, and exercise routines than from each separate digital provider using just the data it holds. People speak of a data commons, but a commons is a type of good that is rival in use (only one person at a time can use it) and non-excludable (people cannot be stopped from accessing it). Data is the opposite, non-rival in use but excludable. Indeed, in some digital markets this non-rivalry is turbocharged by the presence of network effects, which occur when the more other users there are, the greater my individual benefit. An example is an app like Google's Waze, which maps routes incorporating real-time traffic information, much of which is provided by other Waze users. The more of us use the data, the more of us produce it too, and the better it gets. Social media and search are other good examples. More data is often better for identifying meaningful patterns or matching buyers and sellers on digital platforms.

These features are the opposite of mass production, many items that were more or less the same coming off an assembly line. In the digital economy we have massive economies of scale too, but combined with increasing variety and personalisation. For instance, through digital matching platforms like Airbnb, OpenTable, Uber, or Amazon Marketplace, people are able to satisfy highly specific individual needs or preferences. In some cases, no money is exchanged, not only in the case of Al Roth's famous kidney exchange described earlier, but also now the numerous, non-profit sharing economy platforms exchanging unwanted goods or sharing equipment, or dogs.

As with previous episodes of major innovation, from printing to electricity, enormous value is being created. Yet it is not much of an exaggeration to say these phenomena verge on the invisible in the current framework of economic statistics. The advance of the new technologies presents a paradox, one greatly exercising economists at present. This is the so-called productivity puzzle. Labour productivity—GDP per hour worked—or equally the multifactor productivity measuring the increase in GDP not attributable to the use of additional capital and labour—has flatlined since the mid-2000s. Some economists, notably Robert Gordon (2016), see no paradox, dismissing the technology as all hype. Although there is without question plenty of hype, others (including me) are burrowing into the statistics to try to understand better how an increasingly weightless economy of zeroes and ones is being reflected, or not, in the standard economic statistics.

Political Arithmetic

The standard measure of progress, often used to assess economic policy proposals, is GDP: 'real' GDP adjusted for general increases in the price level. This measure of the size of the economy has many flaws, which have been much rehearsed over the seven decades since its invention. This is not the place to repeat them all, but the key point is that its origin in wartime meant the concept of the economy crystallised in a definition that was explicitly *not* a measure of economic welfare. In many countries there has been at least a decade of divergence between growth in average GDP per capita and the experience of many people whose living standards have stagnated or declined. So on the one hand, critics point out shortcomings like the failure to reflect income distribution in the headline figures, arguing that GDP growth over-states gains in economic welfare. On the other hand, a different set of critics, in the tech sector and financial markets, believes the GDP and productivity numbers do not capture the benefits of digital change and are therefore understated. It is clear that the 1940s framework is a poor fit for structures of the 2018 economy, but not at all clear what the next set of conventions will be (Coyle 2017).

Yet even some of its critics make the mistake of thinking real GDP is a measure of something—well, real. Far from it; it is an idea. As Thomas Schelling wrote: '[W]hat we call "real" magnitudes are not completely real; only the money magnitudes are real. The "real" ones are hypothetical' (Schelling 1958).

One of the key challenges in measuring economic progress is precisely how to take due account of this constant innovation, large and small, which Schumpeter (1994) famously argued was the defining economic characteristic of capitalism, as innovation rather than prices is the way most companies compete with their rivals. There are new goods being invented all the time, clearly changing the quality (and even quantity) of life. Yet when we say something like, 'Average income in 1978 was equivalent to $30,000 in 2018's money', this means a 1978 Ms

Average would have $30,000 to spend today, on the goods available in 1978.[3] The concept of a price index is that it measures the change in prices that would keep the consumer's utility (satisfaction of preferences) constant, which implies a comparison over the same sets of goods and services. Unfortunately, there was no price for the iPhone in 1978 and Ms 1978 could not have economised on clothes and bus fares to buy one. In practice, statistical offices use a variety of pragmatic techniques to bring new goods into the price index, and drop old ones.

Even when the goods are merely incrementally improved rather than important and exciting innovations, there is a problem. Two indicators are observed—sales price and quantity sold—but three things are changing, the third being quality. If you can buy less bread for your money (ignoring the artisan sourdough option), it is clear the price has gone up, and vice versa. But we would not want the size or weight of a car to be the only criterion for assessing its price; the embedded technological improvements have changed for the better the character of the transportation service it provides. How can the price index reflect the fact that you get a much better car, or computer, or washing machine, for a given amount of money? In principle, the statisticians can estimate the value of the improvements (using 'hedonic' regressions), but in practice, this is done for only a few products such as computers.

Despite these fundamental challenges, real GDP growth paints a fair broad-brush picture of progress. Economic historians have constructed a millennium's worth of GDP statistics showing living standards creeping up slowly for many centuries, a little faster during the Renaissance, and then a lift-off at

3. With a Laspeyres index. With a Fisher ideal index it would be a conceptual basket of goods, not the actual 2018 (or 1978) basket.

the end of the eighteenth century with exponential progress since then. The chart has come to be known as 'the hockey stick' of growth. Statistics on life expectancy, infant mortality, and health indicators paint a consistent picture of progress (albeit linear given the constraints of biology as opposed to a statistical construct that can in theory increase without limit).

However, the fact that economic progress is fundamentally a matter of innovation means the statistics can probably never tell the full story. It is not possible to capture the quality of life gains from better health care, or the ability to speak to a grandchild across the world for free via an online video call—or the other way when considering the loss of species in once-pristine nature or poisoning of the oceans—in wholly monetary terms. These require a fundamentally different kind of calculus. John Hicks claimed: 'Economics studies facts, and seeks to arrange the facts in such a way as to make it possible to draw conclusions from them. . . . Facts, arranged in the right way, speak for themselves. Otherwise, they are as dead as mutton' (Hicks 1942). Chapter Three argued that on the contrary the idea that evidence and values can be separated is entirely wrong. This is just as true of statistics, economic data. The term 'data' derives from the Latin for what is given, but data are not given; they are made. 'Quantitative records can help us to see farther, but only if we remember what the numbers make visible and what they erase' (Rosenthal 2018). We see what we measure, as well as measuring what we see.

To be sure, data have a relationship with actual actions and their consequences; but they are structured in specific ways by the historical outcome of political choices affecting analytical constructs, definitions, and classifications (Porter 1995; Tooze 2001). This is not mere relativism, for the existence of conventional definitions itself acts as a focal point for the behaviour of the many individuals who constitute society, another example of the self-referential phenomena described in Chapter One. As Alain Desrosières (2002) put it: 'Conventions defining objects really do give rise to realities.' The statistics can thus change outcomes—potentially leading to political challenge, and ultimately even a new framework and set of conventions for defining and thus creating data.

To take one example, defining and measuring inflation is always one of the most inflamed statistical debates, because it directly affects the distribution of resources between different groups in society. As noted earlier, there are genuine technical and conceptual difficulties in creating a price index when consumer habits and the character of goods and services change so much over time. But it is also a matter of political economy. As historian Thomas Stapleford has traced in the case of the United States, the search for an 'objective' cost of living index was an attempt to depoliticize the political, to provide a 'technical' distribution of social value (Stapleford 2009). Should a union demand for a pay increase be met? Should pensioners receive higher social security payments? A price index constructed according to economic science could apparently provide impersonal, objective answers. It could, in other words, disguise the normative as the positive.

When the actual statistics fail to satisfy one side or another in what is really a political debate, a methodological review is sometimes commissioned. One of the best-known was the US Boskin Commission. Its 1996 report, 'Toward a More Accurate Measure of the Cost of Living', looked at innovation and quality improvements in particular to conclude that the rate of inflation measured by the CPI was overstated by 0.8 to 1.6 percentage points a year. The implication was that workers needed lower pay increases, pensioners smaller rises in their pensions, to maintain a constant standard of living, as they were able to switch to new, better, and cheaper products. The report was immediately seen as a political document. 'The commission's findings are being used as a cloak for an economic agenda that will injure lower- and middle-income households,' wrote one prominent commentator, adding: 'Revising the CPI would get the Republicans off the hook of deficit reduction, while simultaneously advancing the interests of business. This, however, would occur at the expense of working Americans and the elderly' (Palley 1997).

A similar contest over the distribution of resources has been under way in the UK recently, in the debate about the use of the Retail Price Index (RPI) rather than the Consumer Price Index (CPI) to uprate certain prices and benefit payments. The two statistics have diverged steadily, mainly due to differences in their methods of construction. Economists believe the CPI to be a more accurate measure, but the RPI is enshrined by tradition and in some cases (such as payments on index-linked gilts) by contract. Chancellors have switched some benefit payments previously uprated by faster-increasing RPI to CPI indexation, saving themselves a bit of expenditure, while keeping revenues such as student loan rates and beer duty linked to RPI. The debate is as bitter as it gets in the world of statistics. There cannot fail to be winners and losers.

Another example of the inherent conflicts of interest in seemingly technical statistical constructs is the choice of a discount rate. This interest rate pits the interests of the future against those of the present; the higher it is, the more the present prevails over the future. The idea of discounting was introduced explicitly into political debate in the early eighteenth century in the context of calculating 'the Equivalent', the English payment to Scotland to bail out its economy at the time of the Act of Union. William Deringer writes: 'It placed almost no value on anything that happened beyond one human lifetime. This peculiar claim clashed violently with many Britons' intuition about what the future was worth to them' (Deringer 2018). The debate about how to calculate discounted cash flows became highly polemical, one of the fronts in the political battle between Whigs and Tories. As the ever-sceptical David Hume put it: 'Every man [*sic*] who has ever reasoned on this subject, has always proved his theory, whatever it was, by facts and calculations' (Hume 1784, 328).

A more recent manifestation of the politics of discounting followed the publication of the 2007 *Stern Review* on climate change. It introduced a far lower discount rate than had been typical in estimating the costs of future climate change damage, with the result that higher estimated future costs warranted more urgent action now. *Stern,* explicitly for the reason that there is no moral basis for discounting the well-being of future generations as all are equally deserving of concern, used a rate of 1.4 percent; in the apparently highly technical subsequent debate, some other economists favoured a more typical 6 percent. This means they place more weight on the well-being of the current generation. If we want to embody sustainability in the economic measurement framework by incorporating assets including natural assets in a comprehensive balance sheet for society, pricing the future through the discount rate is an unavoidable moral choice.

The point of these examples, GDP, inflation, discount rates, is that statistical constructs have distributional implications. They are never only technical. William Petty, one of the founding fathers of economic measurement, aptly referred to statistics as 'political arithmetick'. The separation protocol discussed in the last chapter already breaks down with the collection of economic data, long before any economic theorising or analysis kicks in. The claim to objectivity has helped make economics influential in policy-making. There are economists in all central government departments; there are powerful economic regulators, not to mention the central bank; businesses employ economists to lobby government. So in effect modern capitalism is organised as a result of the outcome of a conversation among economists. Looking around at our economies today, post-GFC, post-pandemic, with vast economic inequalities laid bare, the outcome is not pretty.

The influence of economics is without question being challenged as it has not been for decades. Michael Gove's notorious 'People in this country have had enough of experts,' was a statement about values, rather than about economists' expertise. Plenty of others have joined in the criticism, rattling economists to the extent that a distinguished group started the hashtag #whateconomistsreallydo in a bid to convince social media and the world beyond that what we really do is really useful.

There is no doubt that we need to start with the idea of progress, and how to measure it. The current economic statistics have limited our vision and policy actions alike.

This is partly their age. The industrial and occupational classifications provide startling detail on manufacturing industry and almost none on the services that now make up about four-fifths of the advanced economies. The labour force statistics have missed to a large extent the casualisation of the labour market because they embedded the assumption of permanent full-time jobs being the norm. There have been too few statistics of the kind easily available to politicians and commentators about the distribution of incomes between different groups or the fortunes of different regions.

It is inevitable that official statistics, which have to use consensus definitions, will lag behind changes in the structure
of the economy. The 1885 *Annual Abstract of Statistics for the
United Kingdom* has over 100 pages of agricultural detail such as
crop prices in different market towns or imports and exports of
specific seeds or livestock. It has 10 pages on the totems of the
Industrial Revolution, the mines, rail track laid, cotton mills and
canals. By this time, Dickens had died and it was eighty years
since Blake had written of the dark satanic mills. It wasn't that
nobody knew how the country had been changing. The gap
was filled by parliamentary reports, the Blue Books. In a recent
history of measuring progress in the United States, Eli Cook
describes these ad hoc investigations as 'moral statistics' (Cook
2017). Such investigations can form the basis for policy changes,
but they do not provide the scaffolding for everyday policy in
the same way as regular, bureaucratized official statistics.

In my research with my co-authors on some aspects of the
digital economy, we have looked at the quality-adjusted and
data-volume adjusted price of telecommunications services;
at the scope and price of businesses' use of cloud computing;
at shifts in activity from market to unpaid household activity
thanks to digital innovation; at the sharing economy; and at the
use of contract manufacturers by firms which look like big manufacturers but whose main activity is innovation and services.
In every case, the absence of the underlying data gathering has
been a hurdle, and official statisticians are gradually adjusting
their surveys and other forms of data gathering to fill the gaps.

However, there is more to the measurement challenge than
just having failed to keep up with needing to know how many
people are employed in the videogames industry or what proportion of transactions are taking place in bitcoin. Economic
statistics fit the world into a philosophical framework. The

current System of National Accounts has been described as the 'one of the greatest inventions of the 20th century'. The invention of GDP (or rather its predecessor GNP) has even been credited with helping the Allies win the Second World War by providing them with a more accurate estimate of the nations' productive capacity and consumption needs (Lacey 2011). The framework co-evolved with Keynesian macroeconomics—the model given physical form by the above-mentioned Phillips machine with its pipes and valves. Its focus is current period flows of income, consumption, investment, and trade, and its philosophical basis is utilitarianism. Assets, stocks of savings, are no more than passive reservoirs. Nature is largely absent. Social change in the form, say, of women leaving the wartime workforce or joining the paid workforce again from the mid-1960s, or the spread of higher education, is absent. So too is innovation. All change, for better or worse, has been squeezed into the national accounts framework, or been rendered invisible.

The hunt is on for an alternative framework and system of representation of economic and social progress. Amartya Sen's capabilities approach has significant traction in economics. The 2009 Sen-Stiglitz-Fitoussi Commission on the Measurement of Economic Performance recommended moving away from a single indicator (GDP) to a dashboard; the report did not specific its components, but the Commission ignited significant work in the statistics and policy community to think about life 'Beyond GDP'. A number of countries now have measurement and reporting of well-being, environmental accounts, or broader well-being frameworks. However, these vary substantially, and there is no solid theoretical structure commanding wide consensus, so they are used less than one might have hoped. (Note also that dashboards imply drivers, a metaphor still embedding the top-down, outside the model, perspective.) Policies, and politicians, are still largely judged on their performance—at least by the media if not by disaffected voters—by the conventional metrics.

Giving the idea of capabilities statistical form requires measures of access to assets of different kinds. Nascent work in this area divides the relevant assets into different categories: financial, physical, natural, human, social, and intangible. But there is a long way to go before the broad concepts are all pinned down in ways that can be counted, including measures of access by different groups, places, or individuals. There are some challenges too. A focus on assets embeds sustainability because valuing assets now requires thinking about their future uses. This is not easy to turn into statistics.

A vast social science literature tells us, though, that these assets, in some form, are important in determining economic and social outcomes. For instance, social capital can mean the difference between life and death for vulnerable individuals during a heat wave (Klinenberg 2002). A person's social network affects their chances of finding employment (Granovetter 1973). Companies' stock market value, and hence their opportunities for investment and activity, depends on their reputation and their intangible capital, 'goodwill' being the major asset on many balance sheets (Haskel and Westlake 2018). Economists believe that what we label 'institutions', a shorthand for the forms of collective rules and norms in an economy, are the vital element in development and growth (Acemoglu and Robinson 2012). Yet these concepts do not have a tight enough definition to enable them to be measured, posing a challenge for empirical social science. The same measurement gap exists, to varying degrees, for all the types of wealth that seem to have an important role in determining economic outcomes. If we are to take the theories seriously, and certainly if policy-makers are to act on them to deliver better results for people affected by their decisions, there needs to be evidence to support them, or not—which means pinning down the concepts and developing the statistics.

It is possible to think of other approaches to measuring well-being. There is quite a literature now on the direct measurement of well-being or 'happiness' through surveys or diary methods, and a resulting body of econometric work on the determinants of well-being. These include some obvious results—people hate commuting, like having sex—and some less clear findings concerning the age profile of happiness or the impact of higher education (Clark et al. 2018 summarises). An emerging interest in economics is the use of time, the ultimate resource constraint, prompted by the reallocation of time made possible by digital technologies. Time is arguably a better metric than 'output' for productivity in services, which make up four-fifths of the economy: sometimes saving time improves the service (a bus journey), sometimes extending the time spent (nursing provided in intensive care) (Coyle and Nakamura 2019).

Here Be Monsters

How do we know whether there is progress in a transforming economy is one of the questions I posed; the other is the challenge posed by the structural economic changes to economic analysis.

The financial crisis and its lingering unpleasant legacies mean the subsequent tide of doubt about economics was not at all surprising. The post-pandemic economy will be further weakened, leaving some people facing debt burdens, unemployment, and food banks. The double economic catastrophe in just over a decade is reinforcing questioning of what we mean by economic progress, and the role of economists in achieving it, or not. Meanwhile, further significant challenges loom. One is the process of deglobalisation; mitigating the effects of climate change and biodiversity loss is another.

Then there is growing concern about the next economic challenge: a wave of automation sweeping over so-far unaffected sectors of the economy, including professional services such as law and accountancy. Advances in digital technologies, robotics, and AI are coalescing to alter the shape of work, automating routine tasks and requiring jobs for humans to be repackaged as non-routine ones. At this stage it is impossible to predict exactly what these changes will be, but there are monsters in the unknown territory. Will the 'robots' take half the jobs in twenty years? (Frey and Osborne 2017). Will their owners grow ever wealthier while more people are pushed into badly paid, precarious work?

These questions pose quite a challenge for economists as experts. As earlier chapters have described, there have been significant advances in economic research over recent decades. But we still lack good enough tools for modelling this kind of economy, and certainly are not teaching the next generations of economists how to analyse—and manage—the transformed digital economy. One of the key changes needed in the typical economic approach is a shift away from analytical models. Even with the modern toolkit of uncertainty, incomplete information, 'behavioural' assumptions and frictions, thinking in terms of cogs in the machine still casts a shadow. We want there to be a single best answer, expressible in equations. Yet the characteristics of the digital economy mean outcomes are often self-fulfilling (or self-averting) and therefore indeterminate. This has always been the case as Chapter One emphasised—a recession is a self-fulfilling prophecy, for example (Farmer 2010; Shiller 2019). It is unfair perhaps to single out economics for linear thinking, for ignoring the avalanche dynamics of feedback loops. The experience of the pandemic is enough to demonstrate how hard many people, including policy-makers, find it to grasp exponential dynamics.

One example of how non-intuitive non-linear phenomena can be is a surprising recent resurgence of the debate about the Y2K phenomenon, or Millennium Bug. As the year 2000 approached, it dawned on the computer community that—to save on memory space—dates had generally been encoded as only the last two digits of the year. Many computer systems were going to interpret the year 2000 as 1900, with unpredictable and potentially dangerous consequences, as this feature was embedded in very many pieces of software across many systems that had accumulated different archaeological layers of code over time. As the end of 1999 approached, every day brought screaming headlines about planes falling out of the sky at the stroke of midnight and so on. The clocks struck 12, "Auld Lang Syne" began to ring out—and nothing happened. Had it all been hype? The leading pro-Brexit politician Jacob Rees-Mogg thought so, tweeting in 2018 that there would be no cliff-edge Brexit disaster just as there had been no Y2K disaster. The software engineers were outraged, for of course the reason there was no Y2K disaster was that they had spent two solid years recoding the systems. Disaster is only self-averting if people act as though it will happen.

Another example of the need for a different approach to policy is the Close the Door campaign. As you walk down a high street in winter, you will find many stores with their doors wide open blasting out heat in the entrance. This is not a desirable state of affairs either in environmental terms or in terms of the stores' energy bills. So why do they continue to do it? Their fear of discouraging ambling shoppers from entering their store, when every competitor's door is open, outweighs their desire to cut the electricity bill, or reduce emissions. No shop can shut the door unless the others do so. It is a classic co-ordination problem, and the campaign aims to co-ordinate actions, but cannot succeed until a critical mass of door closers has been reached on every high street. A regulation banning open doors would achieve the same, and more effectively because individual shops could not backslide. But when I tried to explain this to economic analysts in the relevant Whitehall department, they were simply bemused. Co-ordination policies are not a standard weapon in their analytical armoury. Yet at a time when new technologies are producing new products, setting technical standards to align investors and businesses in ways that will create large new markets will be essential. Co-ordination policies can be extremely powerful. For example, the European Union's setting of the GSM standard for mobile telephony in 1987 had, within a decade, led to a massive global market in network equipment and phone handsets based on common standards. The alternative would have been balkanised or competing standards. Eventually, one would probably have prevailed, but at a significant opportunity cost in terms of the cost of building out networks and all the progress that unleashed as mobiles spread in developing economies. We need standards to be set now for areas of innovation ranging from autonomous vehicles to data to 'smart' urban networks.

Most economists will be nodding agreement, but in general there is surprising sluggishness in thinking about policy in any other way than an analytical, almost mechanical, way. A dangerous dog savages a baby—so ban dangerous dogs. How to define them? Draw up a list of the relevant breeds. There is no cognisance of the likelihood that the kind of people who owned pit bulls would cross-breed animals to get around the definition. Set out a list of specific taxable benefits, gold ingots, or fine wines, and the financial sector will move on to paying people in a different form. Perhaps we should blame politicians rather than economists but as discussed in Chapter Two there is extraordinarily little acknowledgement in conventional policy-making of the predictable—whether 'rational' or 'behavioural'—adjustments people will make in response to policy changes intended to constrain their actions. These are often labelled 'unintended consequences' and while they may be unintended, they are not always 'unforeseeable'. In this world of self-fulfilling dynamics and even performative outcomes (Chapter One), it is less possible than ever to sustain the idea that economic experts can stand outside society looking down with benign objectivity, pulling levers.

There is almost a policy-design algorithm: specify a problem; gather evidence and analyse it; design a policy to correct the problem; introduce the appropriate regulation or legislation. This algorithm has been enriched by the introduction of behavioural considerations at stage three, the regularities of human psychology now being admitted at the preceding evidence stage. In practice, the policy algorithm can be retrofitted to justify a choice made for all kinds of other non-analytical reasons, such as ideological belief, short-run political imperatives, changing social norms, power dynamics, media or social media outcries, and the general randomness of the universe. Improving the design of policies—to get better outcomes, however we decide to define and measure them—needs to become more reflexive, recognising that the subjects of the analysis can, like Alice's flamingo and hedgehog, talk back. This means considering, across technocratic domains such as economic regulation or monetary policy, how social norms change, how dynamic phenomena become self-fulfilling or self-averting, how narratives influence these dynamics, and so on. Perhaps policy-makers need to think about the role of leadership and symbolism, and about co-ordinating individual decisions—in game-theoretic terms, about designing the rules of the game (including themselves as players), and setting focal points, rather than incentivising behaviour within a specified game (excluding themselves as players).

If the engineer or plumber metaphors are inadequate, what about the economist as storyteller? Economic statistics are what we use to tell the story of the economy as a whole. Small revisions in the figures—which occur frequently—can change the narrative. One example is the UK's emergency loan from the International Monetary Fund in September 1976, when Chancellor Denis Healey turned back on his way to the airport to deal with the crisis. The trigger was yet more dismal statistics about the twin balance of payments and government borrowing deficits, the latest manifestation of Britain's long post-war struggle with a lack of competitiveness (Roberts 2016). The IMF, inevitably, insisted on large cuts in public spending as a condition of the loan. The austerity contributed to the troubled end of the Labour Government after the Winter of Discontent, and paved the way for Mrs Thatcher and Thatcherism. The latest published figures show the current account and budget deficits were a smaller share of GDP than thought at the time, and also show the economic cycle to be less pronounced than did the contemporaneous statistics. The economy was without question in a mess so the statistics alone probably did not change the course of history—but the counterfactual is striking. Successive revisions to the official GDP statistics between 1996 and 2012 removed three out of the ten recessions the 1995 vintage statistics had recorded between 1955 and 1995 (Berkes and Williamson 2015).

Of course, the same data can be used to tell different stories. When the third quarter of 2014 GDP growth figure was published on the first day of the 2015 UK General Election campaign, 30 March, the *Daily Telegraph* headline was: 'UK economy grew at fastest rate for nine years in 2014', while the *Guardian* went with: 'Data shows slowest recovery since 1920s' (Khan 2015; Allen and Watt 2015). Subsequently, an apparent 'double dip' recession in the aftermath of the GFC has been revised away in the latest statistics.

The idea of narrative economics has advocates (and narratives as an element in policy are cropping up in other domains such as the natural sciences or AI). Robert Shiller (2017, 967) compares economic narratives to epidemics, infections of the mind. He writes: 'The field of economics should be expanded to include serious quantitative study of changing popular narratives,' adding, 'Narratives can be based on varying degrees of truth.' Similarly, George Akerlof and Dennis Snower argue that neither conventional nor behavioural economics offers empirically valid general accounts of the way economies develop, whereas considering the role of narratives can account for the realisation of one among a number of indeterminate outcomes: narratives teach social norms, shape individuals' identities and motivations, and prompt their decisions (Akerlof and Snower 2016).

For those who are made a bit queasy by the idea that economists might set up as storytellers—or less provocatively as interpreters of narratives—there is an alternative way of thinking about the implications of the analyst being unable to stand outside the model. In his 2018 book *The Republic of Beliefs*, Kaushik Basu takes a game-theoretic approach, incorporating the rule-setters and enforcers as players. This approach suggests that the task of policy is twofold: to influence the focal point of the game; and to include the incentives and behaviour of decision-makers and experts in policy design. This takes forward the spirit of Thomas Schelling's work (1960, 2006) on strategic policy design and self-enforcing interventions (such as the traffic light, a rule everyone has an incentive to obey). The game-theoretic approach makes it obvious that the task of policy is twofold: to influence the focal point of the game and to include considerations of enforceability in policy design.

This chapter ends where it started, with the technology. Even at this early stage in its application, AI is forcing an even faster confrontation with the question of what sort of society we want, and doing so in a way that raises profound questions about policy.

The term 'AI' is used in a rather general way, sometimes loosely including all algorithmic decision making. There is a key distinction, though, between decisions that can be encoded in a specific algorithm and those generated by a machine learning system. Some problems may need significant computing power, but how to solve them can be spelt out in step-by-step instructions to the machine. Decisions can then readily be explained. Other problems—more widespread in the policy world—do not have known solution procedures. Why are students from certain schools underperforming? What is causing the obesity epidemic? The economic approach is to set out an analytical model of possible causes and test these hypotheses empirically using econometric tools, but I think it is fair to say that in these two examples, among others, there is no consensus pointing to a clear policy solution. These are complex environments with many potential contributory factors. Machine learning or neural net approaches use minimal explanatory structure and a large amount of data, and have a well-defined objective. They will produce decisions that may work very well in delivering the target, but are inherently hard to explain. If we could have explained the model, then using these AI methods would be less useful. They are most useful precisely where we don't know the answer.

Policy-makers naturally have a problem accepting black box solutions, and for some good reasons. These include questions about the robustness of AI to change in the data-generating process, and about bias due to the data sets. At least as important is the question of legal responsibility or political accountability: are we really going to accept that autonomous vehicles can motor round the streets with occasionally lethal consequences if they are owned by limited liability corporate entities? Will a minister of justice ever be accountable for sentencing or parole decisions if most are made by machine learning systems? How are the trade-offs between outcomes to be encoded in the machine's objective function? Will this sit uneasily with the important role of compromise in politics, which the need for explicit objectives translatable into code may make far harder (Coyle and Weller 2020)? At the same time, the question focuses attention on whether we have the right counterfactual: are policy decisions and outcomes taken now in an analytically explainable way? Or is it, on the contrary, a complex and hard-to-explain process? And in that case, should we place more trust in the imperfect human embedded in society, or in the powerful, genuinely impartial machine?

Above all, what objective functions should be written in code? AI is asking us urgently: what kind of society do we want? For now, the machines are all utility maximisers like *homo economicus*, but on steroids. Algorithms are better than judges at predicting which prisoners should be denied parole, so 40 percent fewer people can be incarcerated and the crime rate reduced simultaneously. If the AI disproportionately rejects parole for black prisoners, and yet reduces the black prison population significantly, is that a desirable outcome? The question forces consideration of the aim of policy—what counts as a better outcome—but also of the wider social system within which decision making is being delegated from humans to machines.

Intermission

Chapter Four asked what does it mean to say things are getting better in the economy? Current events make this a pressing question. Is the disruptive technological transformation we are all living through helping or hindering human progress, taking into account both the tremendous convenience of online services and the evident dark side of social media? What might 'building back better', a common slogan, after the coronavirus pandemic mean?

The economic consequences of the pandemic and the subsequent lockdowns exposed the fractures and pathologies of society—the inequalities, the poor working conditions in so many jobs, underfunded public services, institutional weaknesses in responding to the emergency, so many people's lack of access to parks for the balm of green space or to unpolluted air to breathe. It is a brutal snapshot of the vast need for 'building better', and perhaps that idea of aiming to get back to how things were before is profoundly under-ambitious.

The downturn has therefore highlighted long-standing economic frailties in a number of western (and other) economies.

Since the mid-2000s productivity across the OECD countries has barely been growing. Median household income in the UK had already stalled, while incomes for the poorest fifth actually fell from 2017 to 2019. In the United States, the median did not return to its 2000 level until 2016 and has subsequently declined again.

The disappointing economic performance has a geography too: educated workers in big cities have generally done ever-better, while others have seen their towns left ever further behind. Public sector austerity has reinforced this: the same places have lost many kinds of amenities, from local hospitals to shops and leisure centres (Algan, Malgouyres, and Senik 2020). Health inequalities between places are substantial, with—as it has turned out—ominous epidemiological consequences. The challenge looks daunting, to enable left-behind, rust belt, deaths-of-despair places within the rich countries to catch up to their prosperous places.

The health and economic emergency comes on top of significant changes in the structure of the economy, driven by technology and demography, as well as globalisation and current geo-political reversal. Economists and statisticians, me among them, have been trying to improve the measurement of the digital economy, which is not adequately captured by existing statistics. The current periodic revision of the internationally-agreed definitions, the System of National Accounts, is due to complete in 2025 with revamped approaches to measuring digital activities. The tech-driven changes mean that on the one hand, to take one example, measures of price inflation may miss the many free apps people use—such as taking photos on a smartphone and sharing them online rather than buying a camera and film and paying for developing and printing. On the other hand, the digital economy is also clearly helping drive

major inequalities of wealth and power, reshaping politics—
not for the better—and disrupting many existing industries and
jobs. A good deal of economic research has already focused on
the potential impact of new waves of automation on employment and earnings (Barbieri et al. 2019). Estimates of the impact
on employment range from potentially positive (Acemoglu and
Restrepo 2019) to destroying nearly half of current jobs (Frey
and Osborne 2017). All new technologies arouse fears, until
they appear indispensable; the early days of electricity gave
birth to Frankenstein after all. The Victorians thought electricity would kill them, and it is indeed a dangerous technology.

The pandemic is giving new urgency to debates about how
to understand the changing economy and measure how different groups of people are doing. If we had been using a lens
other than conventional GDP growth during the past decade,
we would already have had a different mental picture of economic progress. We would have been aware of the big differences in income growth between different places or different
socio-demographic groups. We would know how far we have
run down the country's natural capital to sustain lifestyles, by
destroying biodiversity and altering the climate. We would be
more aware of the massive transformation in people's everyday life and in business models thanks to digital platforms, and
also more aware of the downsides. Policy-makers are running
to keep up with these, from tougher competition policy to tame
the power of the digital giants to legislating for privacy and
against online harms, to regulating biased uses of AI such as
facial recognition.

People sense this from their own experiences, and the appetite is there for a far broader understanding of what is meant
by progress, by the 'better' in the 'building back' slogan. Polling during the pandemic suggested almost a third of Britons

said the government should make big changes in the way the economy is run. The appetite for change, with a focus on the health of society rather than the wealth of a few individuals, seems particularly strong among millennials and GenZ.[1]

This is far from amounting to a consensus about what changes are needed. But the fundamental sense of unfairness is palpable. Whatever we mean by the economy growing, by things getting better, the gains will have to be more evenly shared than in the recent past. In particular, the new technologies transforming life will need to bring wider benefits than they have so far. An economy of tech millionaires or billionaires and gig workers, with middle-income jobs undercut by automation will not be politically sustainable. Biotech or medical innovations from 3D printed organs to personalised cancer treatments cannot be the preserve of only the super-rich.

The tech-driven inequalities had already disrupted politics in many countries by destabilising the solid middle. Perhaps the shock induced by Covid19 can ensure that lasting change comes about, or—melodramatic as it feels to write this—we may be in for a revolutionary period.

These next two chapters focus first on how economics as a subject and secondly economic policy-making need to step up to the challenges posed by digitalisation.[2] Chapter Five draws together the earlier themes in this book in the context of the distinctive economic characteristics of digital technology,

---

1. https://www2.deloitte.com/global/en/pages/about-deloitte/articles /millennialsurvey.html.

2. These chapters use material from a lecture at the Oxford Martin School in June 2019, https://www.oxfordmartin.ox.ac.uk/events/changing-technology-changing -economics-with-prof-diane-coyle/ and at Nottingham Trent University in February 2020, https://www.ntu.ac.uk/about-us/events/events/2020/02/professor-diane -coyle-cbe.

explaining why this amplifies the shortcomings in economic analysis. Chapter Six focuses on political economy and how to bring about the fresh approach to policy we need so urgently. It considers some specific policy areas, and concludes with the way the digital transformation spells the end for the separation protocol described in Chapter Three. Economics cannot sustain a claim to be merely technocratic—because if that were true, the economic landscape as I write this early in 2021 means it has profoundly failed. Economists need to think deeply about values and politics; it is being digitally disrupted, along with everything else. These are the issues at the heart of my current academic research at the University of Cambridge's Bennett Institute but informed of course by my interests and experience of the policy world over many years—in fact, over almost a quarter of a century.

5

Changing Technology, Changing Economics

My first book on the digital economy was published almost a quarter of a century ago (Coyle 1997). Engrossed in the research and writing in the year or so prior to its publication, I enthused about the revolutionary prospects of the internet to a very distinguished economist. He replied, 'It's going to reduce transactions costs a bit, but we already know how to handle transactions costs in our models. Why are you wasting your time on this?' He was—obviously with hindsight—wrong. The distinctive economic characteristics of digital technology mean that the way we think about economics itself has to change.

Digital Is Different

'Digital' has become shorthand for ICTs or information and communication technologies. It is an example of what economists denote as a general purpose technology (Helpman 1998), which have the following features:

- They enable radical innovation in products and services and also in processes of production, initially in the innovating sector and gradually across a wider range of activities in the economy;
- They lead to a major re-organisation of the structure of the economy, because they change relative input costs dramatically;
- They require significant additional investment in other areas such as other forms of capital, infrastructure, organisation, skills, and so often start out very slowly, before eventually having dramatic economic and societal impacts.

Printing, steam, and electricity are obvious examples. Paul David (1990) provided one well-known historical account of these characteristics of a GPT, comparing the spread of computer technology in the 1980s to the electric dynamo in the early twentieth century, by way of explaining the 'productivity paradox' Robert Solow (1987, 36) had complained about: 'You can see the computer age everywhere but in the productivity statistics.' While the ultimate impacts were therefore substantial, the impact took a long time to show through in GDP and productivity figures.

Although some economists question whether digital technologies are in the same league as these past GPTs in terms of their broad impact (Gordon 2016; Bloom et al. 2020), my view is that digital will be as transformational as earlier GPTs: eventually talking of the digital economy will sound as strange as talking of the electricity economy. The pace of measured change will be slow, then dramatic. The change in the world is already substantial—although how much better off it has made us all in some more fundamental sense is a question this chapter will return to below.

One way to see just how dramatic the economic rewiring has been is to look at the decline in the prices of goods experiencing significant innovation. The extraordinary decline in the price of computational power (computations per second) through different technological generations has been calculated by William Nordhaus (2015), reflecting Moore's law.[1] The falls in price have accelerated over the years; the cost of computation has gone from prohibitive (massive mainframes owned by the government or big companies) to trivial (a supercomputer in every pocket) since 1950.

When the price of a technology declines so much, people use it a lot more. The falling cost of computation has led to dramatic price declines elsewhere. In my recent research with co-authors, we have found big price falls in some services when the pace of digital innovation is taken into account more fully than in the standard statistics. For example, the price paid for access to cloud-computing facilities has fallen by around 80 percent since 2010 (Coyle and Nguyen 2018). This means that companies that used to invest in servers and other equipment, and hire people to staff large IT departments, no longer need to do so. More and more companies, and pretty much all start-ups, do not make these investments at all now but instead use cloud services such as Amazon Web Services, or Microsoft's Azure. Executives I have interviewed told me they used to have IT departments with skilled data scientists costing many tens or hundreds of thousands of pounds a year, but now for a few pounds on the company credit card they can simply use services provided by cloud platforms, with the latest software

1. Moore's law predicted a doubling of the computer power or a halving of the price every eighteen months or two years. https://www.intel.co.uk/content/www/uk/en/silicon-innovations/moores-law-technology.html, 12 August 2020.

and cutting edge AI. Big firms and government departments and agencies have switched to cloud computing, and new firms start with it.

Another example concerns the price of telecommunication services (Abdirahman et al. 2020). The official price index for these services had not changed much, which astonished telecom engineers as this was a period when communications technology experienced great technological progress: the speeds of data transmission, bandwidth, compression, latency, all improved substantially, while the amount of data people were using and communicating, especially via smartphone, soared. With colleagues at the UK's Office for National Statistics and the Institute of Engineering and Technology, we developed a new price index. Even a cautious version of the new index showed a price decrease of a third since 2010. An alternative constructed by taking the revenue of the telecom companies and dividing it by the volume of data (measured in bits), showed a decline of 90 percent over the same seven-year period. This last is a logical measure because all telecommunications are fundamentally measured in the physical unit of bits. The component services do have different market prices per bit, but they are converging, for example, as consumers switch from costly SMS messages to free WhatsApp or other instant message services. When the cautious version of our new index was used experimentally in calculating the UK's GDP figures, the upshot was an extra 0.16 percentage point a year on growth for several years.[2] This sounds small, but is not when it compounds and is compared to a recent annual growth rate of

2. https://www.ons.gov.uk/economy/nationalaccounts/uksectoraccounts/articles /producinganalternativeapproachtogdpusingexperimentaldoubledeflationestimates /2020-11-02.

around 1 or 2 percent. And this is just the impact of one price index in one sector of the economy.

These are just some of the measurement issues concerning current economic statistics. Measurement is important because it determines how we understand the economy and therefore conceptualise it. GDP is a decreasingly good measure of progress, which is hardly surprising as it was constructed as a metric for the economy of the 1940s (Coyle 2014). In the digital economy, one issue is that GDP is a value-added construct: the intermediate stages of consumption are netted off the final revenues because otherwise there is double-counting: we do not want to count both the flour going into the bread and the bread at the same time. However, this means that the whole process of disintermediation over the last twenty years at least, which is continuing apace with cloud computing and the splitting of supply chains into increasingly specialist activities, is invisible in the GDP statistics. We are netting out all the intermediate stages and somehow the benefits are not appearing in final output. This is a reformulation of the productivity puzzle, and in my view its resolution is likely to involve a rethink of the conceptual framework for thinking about growth.

There is much else that existing economic statistics do not capture. What data flows where and what is it worth? To what extent are companies adopting cloud computing and what are they doing with it? How many are adopting AI? If a manufacturer in the UK emails a blueprint to a contract manufacturer in Malaysia, based on designs by a studio in Berlin, with the IP registered in Dublin, what should be counted and to which country's GDP should it be allocated? What about other prices? The price of a digital camera is recorded, though its weight in the CPI has been going down because people are not buying so many nowadays. But nowhere are we putting the zero price that we're all paying for taking photographs and looking at them on our smartphone. So the price indices that we use to calculate real GDP and real productivity are incomplete (Coyle 2021).

Digital Markets Are Different Too

Amazon was founded in 1994, Facebook in 2004, Google in 1998. Apple and Microsoft are older, getting going in the mid-1970s. These tech companies are bigger than any earlier generation of corporate titans. A handful of them dominate our lives, the big American digital companies known collectively as GAFAM in much of the world, Alibaba, Baidu, and Tencent in China. Other digital companies do not match the titans in scale but are dominant in their activities, platforms such as Airbnb and Booking, Uber, or Deliveroo. As consumers and in business, much of our social, cultural, political, and economic activity every day relies on their services, from online shopping to social media to search to cloud computing. There has been an extraordinary rewiring of life, much of the change occurring since the launch of smartphones and 3G and beyond mobile networks just over a decade ago (Cellan-Jones 2021). Why does digital technology create such concentrated power, just a few giants rather than a varied landscape of multiple digital service providers?

Politics and policy are part of the story but the explanation also lies in a number of underlying economic characteristics of digital markets.

The first of these can be classified as Superstar features. The designation comes from a paper by Sherwin Rosen (1981), in which he explained why particular movie stars or sports stars were paid so much more than all their peers. The phenomenon operates on both the demand and the supply side of the market. On the supply side, there are high fixed costs and low or zero marginal costs, combining to produce substantial increasing returns to scale. It takes years of practice to be a top basketball player and millions of dollars to film a blockbuster movie. Once trained, once produced, the costs of playing an extra game or distribution to one more cinema are low. On the demand side, the goods are essentially experiences: people do not know what they are like until they have actually consumed them—watching the movie or the game. Once people start to hear through their friends and family or reviews that something is good, then—even if by any objective characteristics it is not much better than anything else in the market—demand will increase for that particular star. Superstar features can operate in many digital markets, which have close to zero marginal costs of distribution and are often competing for our attention. They are the first driver of the winner-take-all or winner-take-most patterns so prominent in today's economy.

Another characteristic that tends to encourage concentration in digital markets is labelled 'indirect network effects'. Network effects are familiar: if you want to make a phone call, then the more other people are on the telephone network the better it is for you. 'Indirect' refers to the fact that many digital markets are matching suppliers to consumers, so if for example, you want to hire an AirBnB apartment, the more people supplying the AirBnB apartments the better it is for you. And if you are a supplier who wants to rent out your apartment, the more consumers on the platform the better it is for you. Digital platforms of this kind are also known as two-sided or multisided markets (Evans and Schmalensee 2016a). These indirect network effects are also mutually reinforcing and encouraging of scale. All 'sides' of the platform can—at least potentially—benefit the more users there are on the platform. There are many examples, from familiar consumer-facing ones like AirBnB, Amazon Marketplace, eBay, OpenTable, or Uber to business-to-business ones in industries such as chemicals or steel. Digital platforms also have a particular price structure; if people on one side of the market (usually the consumer side) have more other options to choose from and can switch, then the other side has to subsidise them to persuade them to stay on the platform. As a result, in many of these cases, consumers do not pay anything, and suppliers on the platform, such as advertisers, restaurants or apartment owners listing their apartments, pay a commission or fee to the platform. The commission rates can be high—30 percent is typical, and the rate can be substantially higher in some cases.

A third important characteristic is that these platforms are often matching specific aspects of demand and supply. They are linking varied supply, such as the wide range of apartments (size, location, amenities) you can get in a city, with varied demand, as people have relatively heterogeneous tastes—some want quiet while others prefer to be near the nightlife, some like to be able to cook for themselves, and others do not. The larger the platform, the more any individual is going to be able to make a sale or find the service they want. Again, scale increases user benefits. In the case of consumer platforms, millions or indeed billions of people are getting for a zero monetary price a service they value highly (Brynjolfsson, Collis, and Eggers 2019; Coyle and Nguyen 2020). The digital platforms get their revenues through the commissions charged to the other side of the market, and advertising revenues raised on the basis of using the data they gather on consumers to target the right ads at the most likely customers. Some—including Amazon—process the customer data themselves and sell marketing analytics services to advertisers.

All these features combine to make it hard to get a platform going and make it successful. As four in five platforms fail (Gawer, Cusumano, and Yoffie 2019), it is hard to get to the minimum viable scale, keeping the two sides in an appropriate balance with each other. The big American platforms have very large sums of venture capital money covering their losses for a long period, and those losses can be large indeed. Start-ups can bump along for a while before they reach the critical point, then suddenly they are huge as it all takes off very quickly. If they are not huge, they are generally dead. These are the basics of digital platform economics, and it makes the way the markets operate different from the benchmark mental models in economics.

Digital Economics

In the digital economy both production and consumption are being transformed. The technology has got to the point of indispensability. People are spending considerable amounts of time online. In the UK this doubled between 2007 and 2017, to reach 24 hours a week, one-seventh of what would be possible without sleep. There is other evidence about the high value we place on it. Erik Brynjolfsson asked how much people would need in compensation for giving up digital services such as search or social media for a certain period of time. The average person was willing to give up all search engines for a year in return for about $17,000, which is around half the US median income. For email, the figure was $6,000. In similar survey work in the UK we also found some consumer valuations for zero price digital services far in excess of a market metric such as the average revenue per user earned by providers of the services (Coyle and Nguyen 2020). These are large sums, although it is not clear how to aggregate them or take account of time budget constraints.

As the time spent online indicates, we are doing a lot of things online now—banking, travel agency, education, entertainment, social media, communication, accessing information. Yet much conventional economic theory struggles to account for these activities. This links to the issues discussed in Chapter Three. The construct in economics of individual utility maximization—that individuals have utility or benefit derived from satisfaction of their preferences to the extent possible within their budget constraint, and that individual utilities can be aggregated into social welfare—does not easily allow for new goods, or for enormous changes in relative prices and behaviour. The framework involves an assumption that we know now, or we knew in 2005, what our preference for buying smartphones was going to be in 2019. Yet not only are individual preferences not fixed, especially over future inventions, they are not individual either. The advertising industry has always been based entirely on the malleability of preferences. Now, the ways in which our preferences can be influenced have changed again as social media have become absolutely pervasive. Moreover, network effects mean my utility depends on the choices of others; individual decisions cannot be considered independently.

The digital economy raises questions about some of the other key assumptions underlying the standard economics benchmark. For instance, many digital goods are non-rival. Once somebody has written a piece of software or created a data set, many people could use it simultaneously, without wearing it out. Network effects as well as high fixed costs contribute to the presence of increasing returns to scale across much of the economy. Yet much of the machinery of economic modelling and analysis depends on the assumption of decreasing or constant returns to scale. There are many externalities in the digital economy, as well as network effects, such as the effect my provision of personal data can have on your privacy, if you are similar to me in some ways. You might even question the role of property in the digital economy given how contested matters of intellectual property have become. The battle between John Deere and farmers purchasing its tractors as to who owns these expensive assets is a striking example: they are so software-laden now, feeding data from their operation back to the company and conversely, that John Deere claims farmers are only renting the tractors, whereas farmers claim the right to own as they have previously done (and repair for themselves) a vehicle for which they have paid hundreds of thousands of dollars. A similar tussle applies to autos linked to software and information provided by manufacturers, or to aircraft engines which are serviced in flight by data zipping to and from their makers' service centres.

Some economists reading this will be thinking that there is nothing new in these points. We all know of course that the assumptions do not hold in the real world and are only a starting point to order our thinking about the economy. However, as discussed above, the thousands of economists in government as well as economics students and many researchers have been socialised into the conventional default thinking that the aim of policy is to increase individuals' utilities, that markets are generally speaking the best way to organise the economy, and that specific externalities or other failures of the assumptions can be identified and picked off one by one with appropriately tailored policies.

Having accepted this for many years, I now believe the degree of interdependence and increasing returns in the modern economy means this is incorrect and an unhelpful framework for designing economic policies. Chapter Six will focus on the policy questions. Here I want to consider the implications for economics itself.

A New Agenda for Economics

I am not proposing a revolutionary agenda so much as a reassembly of important but under-used insights. For example, there are examples of economic analysis that take seriously the interdependence of individual choices, or non-rivalry of goods. The area of market design (Kominers, Teytelboym, and Crawford 2017) considers individual choices in the context of interdependence, as does game theory. Some game theorists recognise that the makers and enforcers of the rules of the game are players too, and that social norms matter as much as individual outcomes (Basu 2018; Sugden 2018). With co-authors I have looked at whether there can be an effective market for data (no), and what policies might be needed for the use of data in the digital economy to generate social good (Coyle et al. 2020). There is a rapidly-growing body of research into digital platforms, although with plenty of gaps remaining to fill.

Appreciating the feedbacks, the self-reinforcing (or self-averting) phenomena, is likely to require a different approach to modelling and analysis. There are examples of alternatives already being used by some economists, such as complexity theory (Arthur 2021; Hidalgo 2021), agent-based modelling (Gallegati and Kirman 2012; Richiardi 2016) and connectionism (Schulze 2010). All involve computer-based approaches rather than the algebraic analysis economists have typically used, and are increasingly being adopted in economics—without there yet being a single new paradigm to dethrone the existing mainstream. My sense is that at some point in the next decade that methodological paradigm shift will happen.

Whichever of these alternatives, or others, becomes widespread, what economics must do is take as the starting point interdependence in individual choice, the high fixed costs and increasing returns to scale, pervasive spillovers, and the non-rivalry of many digital goods (which are classic 'public goods', or 'club goods', when excluding access to them is feasible). The kind of tipping-point dynamics that characterise digital markets, or technology switches like those needed for a transition to a low-carbon world, need to feature prominently, with their implications for policy in terms of the role of co-ordination and narratives. There are ample literatures to draw on, such as the older ones on the economics of public goods, or of game theory, as well as the newer ones like complexity or connectionism. What the discipline has not yet done is to mainstream these divergences from standard models as the new standard. As my very distinguished economist said to me at the dawn of the digital economy twenty-five years ago, we can indeed handle a lot of these features in our models. We now need to go ahead and do it, and what's more make this the version we teach to all economics students, and future policy-makers too.

So what is the new agenda for economics in the digital economy? The table summarises the necessary shift in what is taken as standard, the benchmark.

Twentieth- and Twenty-First-Century Economics

TWENTIETH-CENTURY ECONOMICS	TWENTY-FIRST-CENTURY ECONOMY
Linear	Non-linear
Static	Dynamic
Constant or decreasing returns	Increasing returns
Externalities an exception	Pervasive externalities
Evenly distributed	Unevenly distributed
Fixed preferences	Fluid preferences
Individualist	Social
→Bias toward markets	→Bias toward institutions

Some practical and empirical approaches to the issues, from measurement to theory to policy applications such as competition policy, are needed too. How should a competition authority estimate the harm to consumers due to a new search engine not being able to get into the market, for example, and what kind of regulation and governance would make digital markets deliver broad societal benefits?

For economics itself, the agenda is clear. We need to build on the work that already exists to incorporate as standard externalities, non-linearities, tipping points, and self-fulfilling (or self-averting) dynamics. We need to revive and rethink welfare economics (as Chapter Three underlined). We need a modern approach to the public provision and regulation of information goods, applying the rich literature on asymmetric information and older network industries to the non-linearities and externalities of the digital world. And we need to put the social, not the individual, at the heart of the study of economics, taking seriously the line often-stated about the importance of institutions and trust to economic outcomes. This means above all returning to the origins of economics as political economy. The separation protocol discussed in Chapter Three has been a century-long diversion, whose consequence has been to make economics claim a technocratic authority it cannot have, and which events since 2008—both the GFC and the wrecked landscape exposed by the pandemic—have significantly discredited. We individual cogs do not operate separately, as so much economic analysis assumes, and the misleading assumption has given rise to the emergence of collective monsters. Taming them will require recognition of this interdependence, so we can understand, and perhaps manage, the economic challenges the world faces.

6

Twenty-First-Century Economic Policy

Back to the Future: The Socialist Calculation Debate

In his wonderful book *Red Plenty* (2010) Francis Spufford dramatises a heated debate among economists in the early part of the twentieth century, known as the socialist calculation (or economic calculation) debate. The issue was whether the capitalist free market economy or the planned socialist economy would achieve the most efficient outcomes. Which approach to running the economy would triumph?

Some of the most brilliant minds in the field engaged in the debate, including Hayek and von Mises on the market side and Lange and Lerner on the planning side (Hayek 1935; Von Mises 1920; Lange 1938; Lerner 1938). What *Red Plenty* illustrates with tremendous narrative verve is the formal equivalence of the two approaches. The omniscient central planner and the Walrasian auctioneer of competitive general equilibrium theory are identical in the frictionless, full-information worlds of their respective sets of assumptions (Lange 1936, 1937). Both approaches are therefore equally unrealistic, requiring for example, a complete set of markets including for all future products on the one hand or a complete indexing (including by time and place) of all products on the other; and both having immense informational requirements.

As history—and *Red Plenty*—reveal, the market version proves superior in practice because the price mechanism summarises, albeit imperfectly, the information about supply and demand conditions that brings about the allocation of resources to production of all the goods and services in the economy. This is the point made by Hayek in his classic article, 'The Use of Knowledge in Society' (1945). He argued that the information a central planner would need in order to achieve efficient economy-wide production can never be known by one person or organisation. The vast amount of necessary information is decentralised, and the price mechanism can co-ordinate it better than the planner can extract it.

In an extended blog post reviewing *Red Plenty*, Cosma Shalizi worked out the computational requirements for Soviet central planning to have been effective.[1] The problem is formally computable in that the number of computations required increases polynomially rather than exponentially with the number of goods and services; but in the USSR of 1983, even with its limited product range compared to the United States, would have needed a computer a thousand times faster than the best then available to work out an economic plan in less than twelve months of computation. 'Formally possible' does

---

1. Cosma Shalizi, 'In Soviet Union, Optimisation Problem Solves *You*', Crooked Timber, http://crookedtimber.org/2012/05/30/in-soviet-union-optimization -problem-solves-you/.

not mean 'practical'. Increasing the number of variables in the linear programming problem—the number of goods—would increase the time needed by a polynomially greater factor.

Of course, the power and speed of computers has increased in line with Moore's law since 1983, giving new hope to the advocates of socialist calculation. Surely AI can finally deliver us an efficient central planner? Computational economic planning was tried in Allende's Chile in the 1970s, in the well-known Project CyberSyn (Medina 2011). The hope that today's far more powerful computers and algorithms can enable efficient economic planning in place of the chaos of the market has prompted both a modest scholarly revival and less modest hopes for the triumph of communism expressed in popular books (Cottrell and Cockshott 1993; Cockshott and Zachariah 2012; Morozov 2019; Bastani 2019).

However, these hopes will also prove unfounded. Computational speed is just one reason effective central planning remains a distant prospect. Although today's computers are clearly more powerful, and exponentially so, than those of 1983, they have not yet caught up with the polynomial expansion in the number of necessary calculations.

One reason is the increasing number of products available. There are no economic statistics on this. We have to rely largely on the evidence of daily experience, knowing the extent of variety and customisation available now. Consumers can design their own sneakers, configure their laptops in many ways, choose from hundreds of different cloud computing services or dozens of mobile phone packages, eat vegan or gluten-free in high street fast food outlets. The few statistics that are available indicate a massive expansion in new varieties (Coyle 2021). Could a central planner, even with today's computer power and AI, calculate how many vegan burgers versus boneless dip meals will be demanded at each KFC outlet on each date? It seems quite unlikely.

There is a second reason. Not only are there many more products now, needing to be indexed by location (or else a full accounting for transport costs and times is required) and time (for any products that perish or depreciate—last week's loaf is no use); but also the algorithms used require the assumption of linear or at least convex production functions. This technical term means there must be either constant or diminishing returns to production: use a bit more of the inputs needed and you get the same (constant) or a little bit less (diminishing) additional output as production expands.

Unfortunately, increasing returns to scale or network effects mean the real-life programming problem for socialist calculation involves non-convex constraints. As described in Chapter Five, high fixed costs of starting up and network effects in digital business mean there are often these very large increasing returns to scale. As Shalizi observes: '[T]here are no general-purpose algorithms for optimizing under non-convex constraints. Non-convex programming isn't roughly as tractable as linear programming, it's generally quite intractable.' This may be overstating the impossibility, as algorithms manage to address similar problems such as how should a logistics firm collect and deliver millions of parcels across the world; but at the scale of the whole economy with all the varieties it contains, it is certainly challenging. And these non-convex or increasing returns phenomena are pervasive in the modern, service- and knowledge-based digital economy.

The digital economy simply does not conform to the assumption of constant or diminishing returns to scale needed for central planning and indeed for the workhorse models of mainstream, market economics. This was obviously also true to a degree of the pre-digital economy, where after all steel works or aircraft-building involved very large fixed costs and therefore increasing returns to scale. But now non-convexities are absolutely everywhere: software, movies, databases, pharmaceuticals, online retail, even operating taxis.

Economics needs to have at its heart increasing returns and the kind of dynamics they imply. The characteristics of a knowledge-intensive economy are distinctive. While this is certainly a vibrant area of research, it is not yet the mainstream benchmark, and still less so in the lecture hall or the corridors of power. The approach to policy needed in an increasing-returns economy is very different from today's approach, which is still shaped by the 'markets know best' presumption prevailing since 1979 or certainly since the collapse of communism in 1989. Central planning did not work. The recent model of 'free market' capitalism does not work either, and for the same reasons; it has just been slower in its collapse.

A second issue is the assumption made in economics that 'agents', that is firms or individuals or planners, use relevant information efficiently to optimise an objective function— also assumed on both sides of the socialist calculation debate. There has been a lot of attention paid to the cognitive processes involved, yet even behavioural economics assumes there is something to be maximised or optimised, and some underlying 'real' preferences. But we do not always want to optimise an objective function, and particularly as AI increasingly automates decision making, including in sensitive areas of policy. For much economic policy requires constructive ambiguity about the objective function, exactly what it is that is being maximised, exactly because life involves trade-offs and conflicts of interest. Computers do not do constructive ambiguity. The experience of planned economies from the USSR to the public sector to any big organisation is that targets are gamed (as discussed in the context of New Public Management in Chapter Four). Machine learning systems are even more efficient than bureaucrats at delivering the targets they set rather than the true desired outcomes—they automate such gaming (Coyle and Weller 2020).

Moreover, the use of AI to make decisions puts a lot of weight on the quality of the information, the data, fed into the programming problem. Data are, notoriously, biased; as Chapter Four described, economic and social data are crafted—even when they are automatically-generated 'exhaust' data, as this is the by-product of existing social and organisational structures. Whether collected by surveys, like much of the data that goes into constructing output and GDP figures, or web-scraped or collected from sensors, the classifications and analytical constructs are far from the kind of 'objective' data used in engineering programming problems. They shape the way we understand the economy because they portray the only way we can see it. Data bias is a major problem in AI applications.

There is, too, a vast amount of missing data about the state of the world. Sampling error or bias, the character of the data collection, and omitted variables (unknown unknowns) all mean no data can be taken at face value (Hands 2020). Externalities are not priced in the market, so, for example, while there is some information about the quantity of CO_2 emitted and surface or ocean temperatures around the globe, there is no carbon price. Where CO_2 emissions are traded, as in Europe, the market works poorly and the price of carbon is well below what researchers estimate it needs to be to price-in the externality and limit emissions. Why would anybody want a powerful AI, coded to optimise for economic efficiency and growth, planning a level of emissions indicated by a too-low market price?

More powerful computers and algorithms are certainly not yet bringing socialist calculation into the realm of reality. But the reasons for the reality check—increasing returns to scale and the inadequate information basis for optimisation of an objective function—apply equally to the market economy and the mainstream of economics. As noted earlier, market failures and government failures occur for the same reasons in the same contexts. This helps explain the ebb and flow over the decades since the Industrial Revolution of thinking about the boundary between state and market; there is no correct answer, as the mix will shift with economic, technological, and political changes.

This chapter is about what the digital transformation implies for designing economic policies. The prevailing climate of ideas in economics informing policy choices has to change to reflect the reality of today's economy, and the change is just beginning. Chapter Five argued that this will need a change of mindset in economics. How do such changes come about? Past transformations suggest an answer.

Political Economy Loops: Events-Ideas-Actions

What determines how any economy settles on its mixture of state intervention and market processes? As there is no analytical answer to this question—no technocratically-efficient boundary—the outcome must depend on contingent factors. And these change over time. There is a feedback loop between events, ideas, and actions: a crisis or shock to the economy occurs in the context of a certain climate of ideas, which determines how people react and what policies are introduced in response (Figure 3). This changes the path of the economy, setting up the dynamics of the next crisis or climacteric, while

The political economy loop

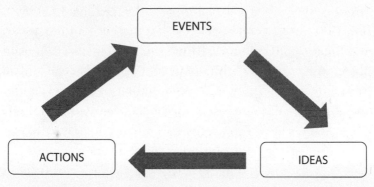

FIGURE 3. The political economy loop

also changing the nature of the ideas that are 'in the air' about the organisation of society. The process has also been characterized as policy-making by social learning (Hall 1989, 1993; Shearer et al. 2016).

There are cycles in technology and finance too, helping drive these dynamics. As Carlotta Perez (2002) documented, historically these follow the same kind of pattern—feedbacks between technological innovations, entrepreneurial ideas, and financial investment—and interact with the cycle of macro events and political and policy ideas. Many economists have been sceptical, to say the least, about any theory positing the existence of long-cycle dynamics since Kondratieff first proposed his famous seventy-year waves (1935), and it is indeed hard to shoehorn long-cycle dynamics into existing economic modelling frameworks. But it is equally impossible to ignore the huge shifts in the prevailing economic philosophy during the twentieth century, occurring alongside transformations in the economic role of government, and dramatic changes in technology. This should not be overstated. As the varieties of capitalism literature and the literature on institutions in economic development both underline, different national institutional structures and cultures have a profound impact on outcomes (Hall and Soskice 2001; Acemoglu and Robinson 2012; Mokyr 2017); Germany or Norway has never looked like the United States or UK. Nevertheless, the broad cycles are apparent, playing into national debates through the filters of specific histories and institutions. Universal trends such as technological change, global events such as financial crises and wars, and the international diffusion of ideas interact with local specificities.

The political economy cycle is evident even in the 100 years since the socialist calculation debate. Both Oskar Lange and Friedrich Hayek spent some years in the 1930s and during the Second World War at the University of Chicago. In 1947 Lange, an advocate of state planning, returned to his native Poland as a member of the Communist government. Hayek remained in Chicago until his retirement back to Austria in 1962, where he was a formative influence on the famous (or notorious) Chicago School, including Aaron Director and Milton Friedman. The Iron Curtain divided the world into planned and market arenas. The Cold War had its economic theatre, the tale told in *Red Plenty* (see also Schmelzer 2016). Both sides competed to claim economic superiority. In Western Europe, Marshall Aid, and the formation of organisations such as the European Steel and Coal Community and the forerunner of the OECD, were designed to limit the appeal of socialism to war-weary, exhausted, hungry voters (Steil 2018). The launch of Sputnik, as well as the nuclear arms race, shocked the United States into massive investment in research and technology, including computing (Waldrop 2001).

Yet despite, or perhaps because of, the Cold War, the climate of ideas in much of the west during these decades was firmly in favour of government intervention. Many European countries set up economic planning agencies. Communist and socialist parties gained high vote shares in France and Italy; in the UK Labour won a landslide majority in 1945 and set about a massive programme of nationalisation and expansion of the welfare state. Keynesian demand management policies to deliver a high and stable level of employment, and avoid the mass unemployment of the Great Depression, rapidly achieved dominion in economics throughout the West. Hicks's synthesis (1937) and Samuelson's canonical textbook *Economics* (1948) codified Keynesianism for the post-war generation of economists.

In this climate even the most ardent free market economists, including Hayek and other founding members of the Mont Pèlerin Society (formed in 1947), accepted a major economic role for the state—although in his famous book *The Road to Serfdom* (1944) Hayek bemoaned the 'entire abandonment of the individualist tradition'. This new society of pro-market economists explicitly rejected the pure laissez-faire of the Victorian era, hoping to carve out in the statist mid-twentieth century a mixed model, with the modest ambition of more space for market forces (Burgin 2012). The experience of Depression and war influenced the intellectual environment created by Keynes among many others, which then shaped the post-war mixed economies of the west. This was the first post-war political economy cycle.

The subsequent few decades brought strong economic growth, thanks in part to reconstruction after the conflict, but also to the active Keynesian macroeconomic policies, and the growth of trade. These were *les trentes glorieuses*, the thirty glorious years in Fourastié's famous term (Fourastié 1979). Electricity in homes and factories became universal, access to cars spread with towns and cities built or rebuilt to accommodate them, while radio and cinema had their heyday. Electricity and the internal combustion engine are examples of general purpose technologies, technologies which can be used for a range of purposes and spread widely through the economy, with substantial economic and social effects. These technologies, invented in the late nineteenth century, delivered the growth and productivity of the mid-twentieth century.

However, the thirty golden years contained the seeds of the next political economy cycle. History is over-determined so there are many possible contributors to the economic crisis of the 1970s. The OPEC shocks, the resulting international capital flows testing the Bretton Woods exchange rate arrangements to destruction, the excesses of public sector unions, all played a part. But so too did demand management policies based on the assumption that the machine metaphor of the flow of incomes around the economy—represented literally in the famous Phillips machine of Chapter Four—was the reality. It turned out that the relationships between economic variables were not mechanical and permanent, but rather were altered by the very policies that had assumed they were. Here again, economics reshaped the reality. So the seemingly reliable inverse Phillips curve relationship between unemployment and inflation—a bit less of one for a bit more of the other—broke down. Inflation increased—sharply so in the UK. At the same time, unemployment started to climb, reaching then-unprecedented post-war heights. In the UK it paved the way for the election of Mrs Thatcher in 1979, after the dreadful strikes of the Winter of Discontent. On the other side of the Atlantic, Mr Reagan won the presidential election soon after, on a promise of inflation-fighting and small government.

The ideas enabling this new political climate, prompted by the economic crisis and a reaction to the previous political and economic consensus, were ready, in the air. Their advocates had been shaping an evolving policy programme for decades, in an international network of like-minded academics and policy entrepreneurs. The origins of the Thatcherite or Reaganite worldview lie in that 1947 formation of the Mont Pèlerin Society, and its bid to keep alive support for a role for markets in the economy when the spirit of the times was so strongly in favour of big government or even socialist planning. Over time, supported by private foundations ideologically committed to the project and prepared to wait for results, the Mont Pèlerin members became increasingly focused on bringing about a purer free market economics, the kind of deregulatory, market-first Chicago School neoliberalism we think of today. By the time of the elections of Thatcher and Reagan, thanks to years of patient and intentional intellectual work, a network of think tanks and academics had a ready-made set of economic policy ideas ripe for implementation (Gamble 1988; Stedman-Jones 2012).

As Steven Marglin sums it up (Adereth, Cohen, and Gross 2020), 'the Keynesian revolution was successful because it coincided with the rise of a new politics: the New Deal in the United States and social democracy in Europe. . . . [T]he Keynesian revolution and the left politics of the period from the 1930s to the 1970s were mutually supportive, symbiotic. Conversely, it's not a coincidence that the demise of Keynesian economics came at the same time as the collapse of the New Deal coalition and social democracy, nor that the politics of Ronald Reagan and Margaret Thatcher came at the time of the neoclassical revival. . . . [T]o effect change you need ideas, but ideas won't thrive until they are associated with a political movement.'

So it was that from the early 1980s the financial markets were deregulated, international capital flows lubricated globalised production chains, governments in the UK and then elsewhere privatised state-owned enterprises, weakened union power, and started eroding the social contract underlying the post-war welfare state. The economy of the 2000s was taking shape, in the process creating the conditions for the next great challenge, the financial crisis of 2008. Financialisation concentrated risk, so the whole vast structure of global finance turned out to be an unstable house of cards. Globalisation meant the consequences were transmitted from one economy to another. There has been almost no improvement in living standards for many households in many countries for at least a decade since then. High levels of inequality are causing political backlash in the context of near-zero growth (Algan et al. 2017; Billing, McCann, and Ortega-Argilés 2019; Pastor and Veronesi 2018). Productivity has flat-lined, alongside this stagnation in real incomes, leading sceptical economists to argue that the current technological innovations are just hype (Gordon 2016; Bloom et al. 2020), and others to focus on the sclerosis caused by market power (Philippon 2019; Van Reenen 2018).

What about the prevailing climate of ideas now, in 2020? The Mont Pèlerin neoliberalism of the 1980s and 1990s, rationalising the deregulation and market-oriented policies of Thatcherism and Reaganism, has much-diminished credibility. Government intervention is edging back into fashion. The response by all governments, even in the UK and United States, to the Covid19 pandemic has emphatically demonstrated their ability to intervene in the economy. Increased interventionism can also be seen in the case some US academics and policy-makers are making for a return to pre–Chicago School antitrust policies, and the breakup of big digital companies; in the revival of interest in old-style regional policies to boost growth in 'left behind' areas; in the debate among European politicians about whether growing EU industrial champions should be a priority to battle subsidised Chinese producers. However, these do not—yet—add up to a coherent framework, and are sometimes attempts to revive the flawed 1970s policies. We are in a period where there are no clear worldviews to shape policy decisions, and there is a mixture of ideas, both statist and free market, combined with profound voter discontent and loss of trust. It remains to be seen whether the crisis now shakes out a coherent alternative.

So is it possible to sketch an economics, and an economic policy approach, for the digital age economy that will respond to the present political economy challenges? The answer will need to take account of the distinctive feature of the economy described in Chapter Five—its non-convexities—and grapple (again) with the centrality of information.

Policy in the Digital Age Economy

Digital has been transformative. The scope of the changes the world has seen ranges from the automation of manufacturing from the 1980s on, and the waves of outsourcing and offshoring, to Tim Berners-Lee's 1989 invention of the Web, to the 2007 confluence of smartphones, 3G/4G, and algorithms that have us all online, everywhere, always. Global production chains, e-commerce, social media, digital platforms, are all made possible by the technological and business innovations. And there is more to come as AI advances, and merges with other areas of innovation such as genomics, additive manufacturing, green energy and transport transition, or advanced materials.

Chapter Five described the economic characteristics of the technology. What have these implied in practice? By 2020 Apple's market capitalisation alone exceeded that of the combined 20 largest German manufacturing firms such as Siemens and BMW.[2] The world of production (Storper and Salais 1997) has been completely reorganised, and to some extent uprooted from specific geographies (Coyle 1997; Coyle and Nguyen 2019; Haskel and Westlake 2018).

One early change brought about by digital technologies was the decentralisation and globalisation of production in multinational supply chains. Starting with manufacturing, progressing to tradable services, multinationals outsourced low-value activities—often to low-income countries—and retained the high-value intangible activities within their corporate walls. At the same time, the corporate boundaries crossed national boundaries while intangible assets were easily shifted to low-tax territories. The driver has been the rapidly declining cost of transmitting information and performing computations. Richard Baldwin (2006) has traced the effects on the international structure of production, describing the 'unbundling' of different stages in the value chain into differently located links, and particularly the separation of ideas from manufacture. Lower communication costs, falling transport costs, and trade liberalisation all combined to make this possible. The costs of information and communication also reshape organisations' internal structures. Better access to information makes it more efficient for important decisions to be delegated while cheaper communication may mean it is easier to refer up for decisions (Bloom et al. 2014). In practice, the decentralisation effect has dominated. Multinationals retain intangible assets at the centre of production networks or—as it is often described—as the dominant member of a production ecosystem.

2. https://www.ft.com/content/6f69433a-40f0–11ea-a047-eae9bd51ceba.

The transformation of production goes beyond conventional outsourcing, and the delayering of corporate hierarchies, however. The scope for reorganising production by combining inputs internal to the firm—capital assets, direct employees, intangibles—with external ones such as cloud computing (Coyle and Nguyen 2019) or a contingent workforce (Boeri et al. 2020) is immense. So too the range of business model choices, taking in standard vertical supply chains but also networks or ecosystems, and a range of platform models (Spulber 2019). Thus the iconic corporate form has changed from corporate hierarchy to networked multinational to multisided digital platform.

An additional driver of organisational change has been the long-term structural shift away from manufacturing to an increasingly service-based and knowledge-based economy. Holmstrom and Roberts (1998, 90) noted: 'Information and knowledge are at the heart of organizational design, because they result in contractual and incentive problems that challenge both markets and firms.' The role of tacit knowledge (that is, know-how that is hard to write down and convey without experience) in a growing proportion of production, and the asymmetries of information pervading many characteristic modern economic activities, mean it is hard to monitor delegated or contracted activities or write legally-enforceable contracts that will cover all eventualities. Although it is easier to monitor the location of an Uber driver or Amazon warehouse worker thanks to digital tracking, or listen in to a call center worker and time their calls, it is almost impossible to monitor the quality of work of a software systems engineer or an accountant while they work and possibly even after they complete it.

It is not even clear what the relevant unit of quantity is: is the volume of a software system really the number of lines of code; or an audit of the number of lines in the financial report? We can tell whether a doctor makes us better or not, but do not know the counterfactual. A teacher can deliver great test results, but only (a long) time will tell whether their pupils are ready for the challenges of the modern workforce.

The digital economy has also rewired consumption. A growing share of shopping occurs online. A growing proportion of services such as TV, listening to music, banking, arranging travel, occur online; while formerly physical products such as diaries, maps, cameras, calculators, and so on have shed their atoms to become bits (albeit still embedded or accessed via a physical device). New types of digital service have emerged. Although it is still impossible to get a haircut without going to a hairdresser, a surprising number of services can be delivered in bit form. This is one lesson of the 2020–2021 lockdowns. Data usage has soared, even before the famed Internet of Things and autonomous vehicles had come into existence, with their data and communication demands.

Zvi Griliches (1994) long ago distinguished between easy-to-measure and hard-to-measure sectors of the economy. Among the former he put agriculture, mining, manufacturing, transportation, communications, and public utilities. Hard-to-measure sectors included construction, trade, finance, services, and government. We might now reclassify communications as hard-to-measure given the scale of technological advance, while manufacturing has declined further as a share of output. The 'measurable' share of the US economy was down to 30 percent by 1990 (from 49 percent in 1947), Griliches reckoned; it is 23 percent now (Coyle 2021).

How should we define price, quantity, and quality in these contexts of ever more intangible output, variety explosion, information asymmetry? Is a smartphone app a low-price camera combined with photo processing? Should we be trying to measure the price of cameras or the price of capturing and storing an image? How should we account for the fact that it is the content of 1MB of data that has value, not the number of bits or the energy use? If an existing pharmaceutical product is applied to a new use (such as oral rehydration therapy, mini-aspirin to avert cardio-vascular problems, or Lucentis instead of Avastin for wet age-related macular degeneration), and nothing changes about costs or production techniques, but health outcomes improve at a lower systemic cost—how should that be accounted for in economic statistics? These are ideas about using existing products in a different way. What is productivity when there are no material products?

These are not simple questions when the conceptual framework for the economy assumes:

a) Price times quantity equals revenue, 'quantity' is
defined, and 'quality' changes little;
b) People have stable preferences for different goods
and services, and there are no new products (or at
least preferences are defined over all future possible
products);
c) Trade involves tangible or at least trackable products
for final consumption.

None of these assumptions holds good any longer.

Policy in the Digital Economy

As noted, the key characteristic of the digital economy is greater economic interdependence. Increasing returns to scale and externalities, such as network effects or data spillovers, mean a choice made by one person or firm affects others.

Some platforms have succeeded in creating economies of scale and scope in activities where there are no inherent increasing returns, by providing a match between consumers and suppliers. For example, there are few economies of scale in the restaurant business, as each diner needs a meal cooked for them, and each meal needs a certain volume of ingredients. Yet platforms are creating economies of scale and scope either through network effects (matching platforms such as OpenTable benefit both customers and restaurants the more of each category they attract to the platform), or through additional organisational innovations (such as the emerging business of 'dark kitchens' (central kitchens serving multiple restaurants) plus delivery logistics. So even in services where scale and scope economies otherwise could not operate, such as haircuts or meals out, digital platforms have created them through algorithms that match buyers and sellers. Digital platforms are also designed to increase the probability that transactions that would not otherwise take place can occur. Apart from increasing the visibility of buyers to sellers and vice versa, improving the likelihood of a match, their fee structures, rules, and ratings systems are all ways of shaping incentives. Platforms have been described as private regulators of the markets they bring into being (Sundararajan 2016).

Many other economic activities now have the feature of high upfront costs and very low or zero marginal costs, including most everyday digital services, but also anything that can be distributed digitally or ordered or organised digitally—software systems, movies or TV shows, online commerce platforms and exchanges. Again, there are plenty of old examples of this increasing-returns cost structure, for operating a steel mill or a power generation plant also involves very high fixed costs upfront and far lower marginal costs of producing one extra unit of steel or electricity. Increasing returns are everywhere now, though. Software is eating the world (Andreessen 2011), and software is costly to write and costless to reproduce and distribute. Almost all intangibles incur costs early, from marketing to build a brand to research and development in creation of new medications or treatments.

Data itself can have large externalities and scale economies (Coyle et al. 2020). Much debate has focused on the negative externality of (potential) loss of privacy when companies build large data sets on individuals for their own tracking or marketing purposes. More important, though (in terms of the contribution to the economy in the broad sense of social welfare, rather than company profits) are the potential positive spillovers that can come from joining up different data. The valuable information content of data is usually relational: for example, the value may lie in aggregating individuals' data to get population information and make predictions; or in combining different sources of data about an individual data subject; or in comparing an individual to a reference data set, such as someone's location in reference geospatial data. Information provided by many different individuals can create useful information about traffic conditions, assist medical research, help manage electricity demand on the grid, or monitor epidemics. The information content of even some very personal data, such as health data, will often depend on aggregated population data.

Interdependence is thus baked in all the way through the digital economy. Scale economies and the importance of big platforms mean ever fewer businesses can ignore their strategic interactions with competitors, collaborators, and ecosystems. One firm's expansion affects all its competitors and suppliers. Network effects mean individual consumption decisions are bound to affect those of other people. 'My' data is valuable to you as well as to Google.

Yet even as the scope of increasing returns to scale in the economy has manifestly grown, interest in the phenomenon among economists has until recently been confined to just certain areas of research. Endogenous growth theory (Romer 1994) puts increasing returns at the heart of the process of growth over time, through knowledge generated in one firm spilling over to others. But this important insight has had a perhaps surprisingly limited impact. In particular, the work-horse growth accounting approach to the measurement of total factor productivity assumes constant returns to scale at an aggregate level. Part of the 'productivity puzzle' is that in the constant-returns world assumed in these growth account-ing exercises, there is no reason for firms to have significantly reorganised production; yet they have. Economists studying digital markets and technology (Arthur 1994) and economic geographers exploring agglomeration effects—more powerful in the modern economy than the old (Autor 2019)—have also necessarily engaged with the kind of dynamic behaviour that occurs in the context of increasing returns. These include tip-ping points and winner-take-all dynamics, multiple possible paths, and the importance of small differences in initial condi-tions or first-mover effects.

It would be a stretch, though, to say such approaches are widespread. In particular, non-convex thinking has not reached the arena of economic policy. The characteristics of the twenty-first-century digital economy, however, have broad implica-tions across many policy domains.

One example already mentioned is competition policy. Digi-tal platforms have features that make it difficult to think about them in the same way as other businesses, in trying to analyse what effect they have on competition. The network effects in these activities, whereby the more users of them there are, the better it is for everybody else on the platform. Many of the digital markets have 'winner-take-all' aspects, and are dominated by a small number of companies—the tech giants—that have successfully taken advantage of the increasing returns to scale feature. Once large, they adopt other strategies that extend their scale and scope advantages. One of these is the strategy called 'envelopment', illustrated perfectly by an example such as Uber Eats emerging from Uber. If you have a lot of users on one side of one market, such as the consumers using your taxi platform, then you try to cross-sell those consumers a completely different product. This is similar to the bundling we are used to in oligopolistic markets with only a few companies. But in the newer digital examples, the products themselves have got nothing to do with each other, unlike a razor and razor blade or a printer and ink cartridge. Uber for example, opted to use its consumers on the platform to provide an entirely different service using the same software and the know-how it has built up about traffic and logistics. This envelopment strategy, very common among big platforms, means that in trying to understand competition, you not only need to think about one market but also all the other ones that the platform could get into. If a dominant company can dive into anything it thinks looks promising, this is effectively raising barriers to entry for other companies in these other markets.

Another striking feature of digital platforms is the data barrier to entry, the vast troves of data big platforms acquire and store about their users. These give rise to a self-reinforcing process, sometimes called the data flywheel or the data loop. If you are a big company providing a great service, you win a lot of customers. If you accumulate their data, you can use it to improve your service, and so win even more customers. The feedback loop is reinforced in the case of advertising-funded platforms by the ability to target ads better, make more money, improve the service, win more customers, get more data, and so on.

What all of these features add up to is that the kind of conventional analysis done by competition authorities has not been helpful in analysing the scope for competition in these markets. In a conventional competition enquiry (I spent eight years doing these in the UK), you look at whether a merged company or a dominant company can increase its price by a small but significant amount and, if it does, what substitution possibilities there are. Can its customers easily switch to something that is very similar, or not? Can its competitors easily start making a similar product? This is called the SSNIP test, a Small but Significant Non-Transitory Increase in Price. However, this test is hard to apply to digital markets, where even the boundaries are difficult to identify because of envelopment. The asymmetry in pricing means that a perfectly competitive platform may still be charging a zero price to its consumers. Analysing profitability is not a useful alternative. Conventionally, if a company has market power, you would expect it to have higher than average profitability. Digital companies, however, can be losing money even when they are very large; and when they do make a profit, they need the profit to be high to cover the initial phase of investors' losses.

Traditional competition analysis, therefore, does not yet quite know what to do with these companies, although across the US, EU, UK, and other jurisdictions the authorities are racing to change their practices. And some people would ask what is the problem at all, if these companies are losing money and charging zero prices? The answer is that the harm in, say, Google's dominance, is that it stifles innovation, preventing newer and better search engines from ever entering the market. This does not mean that digital overthrow does not happen. Facebook's victory over MySpace is one example. However, entry now is harder than it was in those distant days of 2008.

The kind of dynamic analysis that is needed—of competition for the market rather than in the market, to use the economic terminology—is difficult for competition authorities because it involves predicting what might happen to the sector in the future. It is, to say the least, difficult to forecast what company with a better technology might appear to challenge the digital giants, not to mention the consumer response to that technology. History is littered with technology forecasts that look laughable with hindsight. But this is the policy challenge economists have to try to answer now (Coyle 2019b).

Concern about the dominance of some large digital companies has been increasing in many countries. The European Commission has been particularly active in pursuing some of the cases, and even the previously laggardly American antitrust authorities and politicians are now getting interested, particularly since the inauguration of President Biden. A number of policy reports (Furman et al. 2019; Crémer, de Montjoye, and Schweitzer 2019; Scott-Morton et al. 2019) have noted that competition analysis needs to reflect the dynamics of network effects in digital markets, and to address the barrier to entry created by the data feedback loop: more data means both better information about customers and more ad revenue, so services can be improved, which brings more customers and more data. Competition authorities such as the UK's Competition and Markets Authority (CMA) or Germany's Bundeskartellamt have begun to adapt their approach to digital markets, for example, becoming more sceptical about proposed mergers. The CMA concluded that the dominance of digital advertising markets by Facebook and Google means the £500 a year cost of advertising to each of the 27.6 million UK households in higher prices for the advertised products is more than it would be in a competitive market. New regulations are likely to follow, for example, mandating some open-standards data access or enforcing codes of conduct concerning digital platforms 'self-preferencing' their own services when presenting search results, or concerning terms and conditions and APIs.

These moves sit within the current framework of competition economics, with its broad focus on consumer welfare. This is a more or less universal, technocratic analytical framework, albeit deployed differently in different jurisdictions with different legal and intellectual traditions. Some critics of the digital giants would rather ditch that economic framework altogether in favour of a deliberate shaping of industrial structure to limit private power (e.g., Khan 2017). While this makes economists uncomfortable, as it appeals to a political analysis rather than a technocratic one, it is difficult to argue persuasively against it when standard welfare economics cannot easily analyse consumer welfare in the context of network spillovers, lock-in, and non-linearities. The political dynamics are clear—the political economy cycle is responding to increased market power and the consequent political influence of big companies by making regulatory interventions and tougher competition policy inevitable. However, the economic analysis of digital markets is a work in progress. Even taking the consumer welfare standard as the right approach, there is no settled view about how to assess consumer welfare in these winner-take-all markets with many losers, tipping points, and complex ecosystems. As it happens—because of the scale of their domestic markets— the big digital companies are all American or Chinese. So geopolitics is intruding. This means the return of a debate about whether these foreign corporations can be allowed to operate freely in each other's territories, or whether Europe needs its own national digital champions, long after the Reagan and Thatcher revolutions seemed to have buried state economic activism. Competition policy is a good example of an arena of once entirely technocratic economic policy where political economy considerations have become unavoidable.

Another example is industrial policy. Since the early 1980s, under the sway of free market ideas and the evidence of many 1970s disasters, most economists have instinctively opposed industrial policies. These have been portrayed as 'picking winners' who turn out to be bound to fail. Now, the climate of ideas is definitely warming up toward intervention, given the persistent slow productivity and income growth, and the pattern of anti-establishment voting in 'left behind' areas. Among the many reasons certain areas or towns have fared badly is the fact that the pattern of public investment and policies have amplified agglomeration forces. Although this certainly reflects political choices of the past, the economists' standard cost-benefit analysis (CBA) may be another culprit (Coyle and Sensier 2020). CBA techniques are designed to assess small investments. They should not be used to assess any investment large enough to have spillover effects. For instance, a CBA on one new rail line will miss the network externalities generated if the line fills in the system in ways that increase growth, such as new commuting patterns or business connections. Comparing CBAs across rich and poor regions will also tend to favour the rich—even if national average wage rates and land prices are used—simply because additional economic activity is more productive in the already more-productive areas due to the usual agglomeration spillovers.

A few voices in the economics profession have long argued the need for industrial policies to take a strategic view about where the economy needs to go and what capabilities are required (Rodrik 2004; Tassey 2014). In an economy characterised by non-linear dynamics and multiple equilibria, strategic interventions can make a big difference to the path the economy takes—paths that will increasingly diverge from any counterfactual. Aligning people's behaviour to deliver a particular path makes narratives about the economy important (Shiller 2019), much as these are sometimes mocked—like Harold Wilson's 'White Heat of Technology' or Tony Blair's 'Cool Britannia'. The modern update is that government industrial policies should be 'mission driven' (Mazzucato 2013). Although these are slogans, perhaps such approaches do help serve the co-ordinating function needed for successful industrial policies.

A third policy example concerns data. As data is the crystallised form of information, it is always fundamental to the economy, but it is increasingly the embodiment of economic transactions. There is scant data—ironically—about data use, but the available figures suggest it is soaring. The old market framing of the data economy sees the policy questions as concerning individual ownership and exchange: for example, should big companies pay me for my data (Arrieta-Ibarra et al. 2018)? Yet data is awash with spillovers or externalities, has zero marginal cost, and has value highly dependent on context—like water, its use value and marginal cost can diverge widely. We have barely begun to think about data policies that will use this resource as efficiently as possible and create maximum social welfare (Coyle and Diepeveen 2021). Policy-makers know they need to understand the uses and potential of data, as well as the abuses in terms of privacy, but the research in this case lags behind the need.

The fundamental problem for setting economic policies in the digital economy is that there is no settled framework for assessing social welfare in the context of all the non-convexities (and see also Chapter Three). How should policy-makers judge whether or not a certain policy will lead to better outcomes, in some reasonably well-defined sense? Economics has—for now—only limited answers. Economists have become experts at answering narrow policy questions with ever-better empirical approaches and bigger data sets; applied microeconomics is in fine fettle. But there are few persuasive approaches to pressing political questions such as how to tackle the increasing gaps between prosperous cities and poor towns, how to keep a winner-take-all economy innovative and competitive, how to ensure the gains from economic growth are more fairly shared.

Economists need to start providing policy-makers with guidance for an increasing returns economy. But—to return to the socialist calculation debate with which this chapter started—a bias toward government solutions is no answer. The idea that clever people in the centre can now have big enough data to solve such big problems remains illusory.

As Chapter Five concluded, elements of the necessary new analytical framework are available in the economic literature— much of it provided by a crop of Nobel laureates such as Krugman (1991), Romer (1994), Stiglitz (2014, with B Greenwald), and Tirole (1988, 2016). Their work has shown different limitations of the fundamental assumptions underpinning the bias toward market solutions. I do not know what the next paradigm in economics will look like, but it will have as default assumptions increasing returns to scale, information asymmetries, pervasive network effects and externalities, principal-agent relations, interaction between decision-makers—all the many characteristics of the digital economy that do feature in many economic models and areas of specialism, but have not been integrated, or mainstreamed to the extent they shape the current climate of ideas.

Economics now needs both theory and evidence about what actions, by governments or others, will lead to better outcomes when both governments and markets are bound to fail. Remember that non-convex calculations are generally intractable. There is not likely to be a single 'correct' way to manage the economy. Context will matter, and not so much because universal trends are refracted through local institutions but rather because there will not be universal analytical answers to policy challenges. So addressing the challenge will turn economists back from technocrats to political economists, who will need to know their history as well as their Python programming. This will be uncomfortable for many practitioners of this most insular of social sciences but the economy—and the politics—of the present moment are forcing it on us.

Afterword

The upshot is that economics—for all its merits—needs to change if it is to continue making as many useful contributions as possible to policy, and to serving the public. Economists are influential in government (and business), yet are not able to address in practical ways some of the important challenges raised by the transformation of the modern economy. The themes raised throughout this book, in the context of digitalisation on the one hand and populism on the other, have been:

- The need for economists, especially those working in policy roles, to take more account of the way their own actions change the economy—whether by the possibly rare examples of 'performativity', the reflexive nature of people's reactions to policy interventions changing the policy that is needed, or more broadly by shaping a climate of ideas that affects norms of behaviour;
- Acceptance that the 'is' and the 'ought' cannot ultimately be separated, and that while we should always aim to be impartial and evidence-based, economists are

themselves powerful, and yet often unaccountable, political actors in an increasingly technical society;

- In particular, policy economics claims to be making things better, acting in the public interest, so more careful thought needs to be given to what 'better' means and for whom. This is a question of the legitimacy of economists given their role in modern states, and requires a reinvigoration of the field of welfare economics. This is especially so in the context of a digital transformation driving a growing wedge between the kinds of economic statistics available and society's well-being, due to the greater scope of classical 'market failures' such as increasing returns, externalities, and public goods;

- Finally, the need to assemble the building blocks available in much existing economic research into a benchmark framework appropriate to the digital economy, and to provide suitable policy tools reflecting the framework.

It will be apparent that I do not think that this shift is much in evidence, even though there are indeed building blocks available, particularly in sub-fields such as industrial organisation and market design, information economics, or growth theory. However, although the blocks are there, they have not been assembled into a consistent structure and above all do not address the welfare economics questions. Nor are there the kinds of models, tools, and rules of thumb needed to translate these insights into the classroom and the offices of policy analysts. This is why in my own research I investigate the nuts and bolts of economic statistics, consider practical policy tools for digital and data markets, and—through my book *Markets, State and People* and my contribution to CORE's The Economy (www.core-economy.org)—invest in what we teach the next generations of policy-makers.

Public debate about economics at present features loud criticisms, both valid and (quite often) not. There is also a polarisation in some areas of economics as in so many aspects of life now: between free-marketeers doubling down—for instance in the 'Singapore on Thames' vision of buccaneering free trade post-Brexit or the Trump administration's view that tax cuts for the rich will stimulate more enterprise—and a new interventionism.

Yet despite the often noisy debate I am convinced that a changed 'mainstream' paradigm is needed and will emerge. The reason? Events. Digital technologies have fundamentally and permanently changed economic structures in both consumption and production. Globalisation may well be partly unwound, but the technologies will not be undiscovered or unused. And then there is the dual hit of the 2008 financial crisis and the 2020 coronavirus crisis. As I write this, it is not yet clear how severe the economic impact of the latter will eventually be, but it will potentially permanently change public expectations of the role of the state. It is surprising that so little changed in the way the global economy has operated after the shock of 2008–2009. It may well turn out that, like a cartoon character that continues running for a while beyond the edge of the cliff, the consequences were yet to come. The two shocks combined cannot fail to have a lasting effect, just as the Depression and the Second World War did almost a century ago.

Economists now need to step up to the challenge, addressing the internal shortcomings of the profession in its lack of inclusion and diversity, and narrowness of thinking. Political economy is reawakening: an analytically robust, empirically grounded, historically aware, outward-looking and engaged discipline, making a positive contribution to society—as all social sciences should. This is what so many of us wanted economics to be when we chose to study it.

There are some promising signs, in addition to the change that has already taken place within economics. The profession's response to the coronavirus pandemic has been extraordinarily fast and constructive. This includes in the UK the creation of the Economics Observatory, ECO, which synthesises all the research evidence (and gaps) relating to questions policy-makers and the public ask about the pandemic. From first discussions in April, it was launched on 1 June and had posted 100 articles summarising a vast amount of old research and new Covid19-related research by mid-August. Similar co-operative initiatives occurred across the global economics profession.

What about the internal challenges, described in the Introduction? The Black Lives Matter protests in 2020 put real energy into the debate, both about the lack of diversity among economists and the monoculture of the top journals and departments. But the energy will need to be sustained to bring about significant and lasting culture change. As I have argued through this book, economics and economists shape the economy and society through their ideas and their influence on policy decisions. Would a more diverse and inclusive discipline contribute to changing the nature of the economy in positive ways? It would certainly lead to different research and data, raising questions that might otherwise go unasked, questions that lie outside the experience and frame of reference of the typical white, male, affluent economist. Economists also need to work far more with people from other disciplines, such as the other social sciences and humanities for contextual and historical insight, and areas such as computer science and engineering to get to grips with the digital economy.

I veer between optimism about the signs of change and pessimism about the scale of what is needed. In a way, the pandemic response has shown the economics profession at its best, working across disciplines and highlighting the emerging inequalities and challenges as the economy everywhere has tanked. More of this is needed, though, across all areas of policy. If we are to deserve our place at the centre of government and policy, described in Chapter One, we still need to achieve the paradigm shift sketched in the later chapters of this book; and that is never a tidy or easy process.

February 2021

ACKNOWLEDGEMENTS

This book spans a decade of work so there are many people to whom I owe thanks, more than I can list here.

These include: Professor Roger Cashmore, then Principal of Brasenose College, Oxford, for inviting me to give the 2012 Tanner Lectures on Human Values and Professor Alan Bowman, his successor, for hosting them; and also the distinguished panel commenting on the lectures, Kate Barker, Peter Oppenheimer, David Ramsden, and Peter Sinclair; ProBono Economics for the invitation to give its annual lecture the following year; the Society for Economic Methodology, the Oxford Martin School and Nottingham Trent University similarly for their invitations to give public lectures. At the University of Cambridge, my colleagues Michael Kenny and Helen Thompson were especially generous in their comments on drafts of my Inaugural Lecture.

Over these years I have been lucky in my colleagues and students at the University of Manchester and the University of Cambridge, and also in the economists and officials I worked with in different policy roles including the BBC Trust, Migration Advisory Committee, Natural Capital Committee, National Infrastructure Commission, the Digital Competition Expert Panel chaired by Jason Furman, the Competition and Markets Authority, and also as a Fellow of the Office for National Statistics. I count my blessings when thinking of the range of experiences and insights I have gained from these roles and from my earlier, varied, career. The lectures also reflect work with wonderful co-authors: Mo Abdirahman, Stephanie Diepeveen, Richard Heys, Penny Mealy, Cahal Moran, Leonard Nakamura, David Nguyen, Marianne Sensier, Will Stewart, Manuel Tong, Adrian Weller, Timothy Yeung.

I am grateful to many other colleagues in Cambridge and beyond for their comments and conversations helping stimulate my thinking at various stages through the years, including Matthew Agarwala, Anna Alexandrova, Eric Beinhocker, Tim Besley, Sam Bowles, John Bowers, Erik Brynjolfsson, Wendy Carlin, Vasco Carvalho, Jagjit Chadha, Carol Corrado, Jacques Crémer, Meredith Crowley, Partha Dasgupta, Mark Fabian, Marco Felici, Amelia Fletcher, Jason Furman, Tim Gardam, Rachel Griffith, Dennis Grube, Andrew Haldane, Jonathan Haskel, Cameron Hepburn, Cecilia Heyes, Bill Janeway, Dale Jorgenson, Saite Lu, Derek McAuley, Philip Marsden, David Miles, John Naughton, Jennifer Rubin, David Runciman, Paul Seabright, Margaret Stevens, Joseph Stiglitz, Jeni Tennison, Alex Teytelboym, Jean Tirole, Flavio Toxvaerd, Romesh Vaitilingam, Bart Van Ark, Tony Venables, Anna Vignoles, Dimitri Zenghelis.

The biggest single influence on my economics career has been Professor Peter Sinclair, my undergraduate tutor at Brasenose College, Oxford, and a lifelong mentor and friend. He is the reason I became an economist, and he shaped the kind of economist I became. He had an extraordinary influence over generations of students. His death early in the Covid19 pandemic was a tragic loss.

Finally, special thanks to Yamini Cinamon Nair, Annabel Manley and Julia Wdowin for their research assistance; Lindsay Fraser for editing the first draft; Sarah Caro, Hannah Paul and Josh Drake for their outstanding editorial stewardship of the text, and the rest of the outstanding Princeton University Press team; and as always to Rory Cellan-Jones for his constant encouragement and to Cabbage for her company as I worked.

REFERENCES

Abdirahman, M., D. Coyle, R. Heys, and W. Stewart, 2020, 'A Comparison of Approaches to Deflating Telecommunications Services Output', *Economie & Statistique*, Vols. 517-518-51, pp. 103–122.

Acemoglu, Daron, and Pascual Restrepo, 2019, 'Automation and New Tasks: How Technology Displaces and Reinstates Labor', *Journal of Economic Perspectives*, 33 (2): 3–30.

Acemoglu, D., and J. Robinson, 2012, *Why Nations Fail: The Origins of Power, Prosperity, and Poverty*, London: Profile Books.

Adereth, Maya, Shani Cohen, and Jack Gross, 2020, 'Economics, Bosses, and Interest', *Phenomenal World*, 8 August, https://phenomenalworld.org/interviews/stephen -marglin.

Akerlof, George A., 2020, 'Sins of Omission and the Practice of Economics', *Journal of Economic Literature*, 58 (2), 405–418.

Akerlof, George, and Rachel Kranton, 2010, *Identity Economics*, Princeton, NJ: Princeton University Press.

Akerlof, G. A., and D. J. Snower, 2016, 'Bread and Bullets', *Journal of Economic Behavior & Organization*, 126, 58–71.

Algan, Y., S. Guriev, E. Papaioannou, and E. Passari, 2017, 'The European Trust Crisis and the Rise of Populism', Brookings Papers on Economic Activity, Fall, 309–382.

Algan, Y., C. Malgouyres, and C. Senik, 2020, 'Territoires, bien-être, et politiques publiques', *Conseil d'analyse economique*, no. 55, January, 1–12.

Allen, K., and N. Watt, 2015, 'Living Standards Key to UK Election as Data Shows Slowest Recovery since 1920s', *The Guardian*, 31 March, https://www.theguardian .com/business/2015/mar/31/uk-gdp-growth-revised-up-to-06.

Amadxarif, Zahid, James Brookes, Nicola Garbarino, Rajan Patel, and Eryk Walczak, 2019, 'The Language of Rules: Textual Complexity in Banking Reforms, Bank of England Staff Working Paper No. 83, https://www.bankofengland.co.uk/working -paper/2019/the-language-of-rules-textual-complexity-in-banking-reforms.

Anand, P., and J. Leape, 2012, 'What Economists Do and How Universities Might Help', in Diane Coyle (ed.), *What's the Use of Economics?*, London: London Publishing Partnership, 15–20.

Anderson, Elizabeth, 1993, *Value in Ethics and Economics*, Cambridge, MA: Harvard University Press.

Andreessen, M., 2011, 'Why Software Is Eating The World', *Wall Street Journal*, August 20, https://www.wsj.com/articles/SB10001424053111903480904576512250915629460.

Angrist, Joshua, Pierre Azoulay, Glenn Ellison, Ryan Hill, and Susan Feng Lu, 2020, 'Inside Job or Deep Impact? Extramural Citations and the Influence of Economic Scholarship', *Journal of Economic Literature*, 58 (1), 3–52.

Angrist, Joshua, Pierre Azoulay, Glenn Ellison, Ryan Hill, and Susan Feng Lu, 2017, 'Economic Research Evolves: Fields and Styles', *American Economic Review*, 107 (5), 293–297.

Anthony, Sebastian, 2016, 'The Secret World of Microwave Networks', *Ars Technica*, https://arstechnica.com/information-technology/2016/11/private-microwave-networks-financial-hft/, accessed 4 August 2020.

Arrieta-Ibarra, Imanol, Leonard Goff, Diego Jiménez-Hernández, Jaron Lanier, and E. Glen Weyl, 2018, 'Should We Treat Data as Labor? Moving beyond "Free"', *AEA Papers and Proceedings*, 108, 38–42.

Arrow, K., 1950, 'A Difficulty in the Concept of Social Welfare', *Journal of Political Economy*, 58 (4), 328–346.

Arthur, Brian, 2014, *Complexity and the Economy*, Oxford: Oxford University Press.

Arthur, W. Brian, 1994, *Increasing Returns and Path Dependence in the Economy*, Ann Arbor: University of Michigan Press.

Arthur, W. B., 2021, 'Foundations of Complexity Economics', *National Reviews Physics*, 3, 136–145, https://doi.org/10.1038/s42254-020-00273-3.

Athey, S, 2017, 'Beyond Prediction: Using Big Data for Policy Problems', *Science*, 355, 483–485.

Atkinson, A., 2001, 'The Strange Disappearance of Welfare Economics', *Kyklos*, 54, 193–206.

Aumann, Robert J., 2008, 'Rule-Rationality versus Act-Rationality', Discussion Paper Series dp497, The Federmann Center for the Study of Rationality, the Hebrew University, Jerusalem.

Auriol, Emmanuelle, Guido Friebel, and Sacha Wilhelm, 2020, 'Women in European Economics', in Shelly Lundberg (ed.), *Women in Economics*, London: VoxEU, 26–30.

Austin, J., 1962, *How to Do Things With Words*, Oxford: Clarendon Press.

Autor, David H., 2019, 'Work of the Past, Work of the Future', *AEA Papers and Proceedings*, 109, 1–32.

Axtell, R., and Epstein, J. M., 1996, *Growing Artificial Societies: Social Science from the Bottom Up*, Washington, DC: Brookings Institution Press.

Bajgar, Matej, Giuseppe Berlingieri, Sara Calligaris, Chiara Criscuolo, and Jonathan Timmis, 2019, 'Industry Concentration in Europe and North America', OECD Productivity Working Papers, No. 18, Paris: OECD Publishing, https://doi.org/10.1787/2ff98246-en.

Baldwin, R., 2006, 'Globalisation: The Great Unbundling(s)', *Economic Council of Finland,* 20 (3): 5–47.

Bank for International Settlements, 2010, 'Triennial Central Bank Survey of Foreign Exchange and Derivatives Market Activity in 2010 — Final Results', https://www.bis.org/publ/rpfxf10t.htm.

Bannerjee, Abhijit, and Esther Duflo, 2019, *Good Economics for Hard Times: Better Answers to Our Biggest Problems*, New York: Public Affairs.

Barbieri, L., C. Mussida, M. Piva, and M. Vivarelli, 2019, 'Testing the Employment Impact of Automation, Robots and AI: A Survey and Some Methodological Issues', in K. Zimmermann (ed.), *Handbook of Labor, Human Resources and Population Economics*, Cham: Springer, 27. An earlier version of this paper is https://www.iza.org/publications/dp/12612/testing-the-employment-impact-of-automation-robots-and-ai-a-survey-and-some-methodological-issues.

Bastani, A., 2019, *Fully Automated Luxury Communism*, New York: Verso Books.

Basu, Kaushik, 2018, *The Republic of Beliefs*, Princeton, NJ: Princeton University Press.

Bateson, G., 2000, *Steps to an Ecology of Mind: Collected Essays in Anthropology, Psychiatry, Evolution, and Epistemology*, Chicago: University of Chicago Press.

Bator, Francis M., 1958, 'The Anatomy of Market Failure', *The Quarterly Journal of Economics*, 72 (3), 351–379.

Bauman, Yoram, and Elaina Rose, 2011, 'Selection or Indoctrination: Why Do Economics Students Donate Less than the Rest?', *Journal of Economic Behavior & Organization*, 79 (3), 318–327.

Baumol, W. J., 1946–1947, 'Community Indifference', *Review of Economic Studies*, 14 (1), 44–48.

Baumol, W. J., 1952, *Welfare Economics and the Theory of the State*, The London School of Economics and Political Science, London: Longmans, Green & Co.

Becker, G. S., 1962, 'Irrational Behavior and Economic Theory', *Journal of Political Economy*, 70 (1), 1–13.

Becker, G., 1965, 'A Theory of the Allocation of Time', *The Economic Journal*, 75 (299), 493–517.

Bell, D., 1973, *The Coming of Post-Industrial Society*, New York: Basic Books.

Bergson, A, 1938, 'A Reformulation of Certain Aspects of Welfare', *The Quarterly Journal of Economics*, 52 (2), 310–334.

Berkes, E., and S. Williamson, 2015, 'Vintage Does Matter, The Impact and Interpretation of Post War Revisions in the Official Estimates of GDP for the United Kingdom', https://www.measuringworth.com/datasets/UKdata/UKGDPs.pdf, accessed 19 October 2018.

Besley, T., 2013, 'What's the Good of the Market? An Essay on Michael Sandel's *What Money Can't Buy*', *Journal of Economic Literature*, 51 (2), 478–495.

Besley, T., and T. Persson, 2012, *Pillars of Prosperity: The Political Economics of Development Clusters*, Princeton, NJ: Princeton University Press.

Bhalla, J., 2013, 'What Rational Really Means', MIND Guest Blog, 17 May 2013, https://blogs.scientificamerican.com/mind-guest-blog/what-rational-really-means/.

Billing, Chloe, Philip McCann, and Raquel Ortega-Argilés, 2019, 'Interregional Inequalities and UK Sub-National Governance Responses to Brexit', *Regional Studies*, 53 (5), 741–760, doi: 10.1080/00343404.2018.1554246.

Binmore, K., and P. Klemperer, 2002, 'The Biggest Auction Ever: The Sale of the British 3G Telecom Licences', *The Economic Journal*, 112 (478), C74–C96.

Blackaby, David, and Jeff Frank, 2000, 'Ethnic and Other Minority Representation in UK Academic Economics', *The Economic Journal*, 110 (464), F293–F311.

Bloom, N., Z. Cooper, M. Gaynor, S. Gibbons, S. Jones, A. McGuire, R. Moreno-Serra, C. Propper, J. Van Reenen, and S. Seiler, 2011, 'In Defence of Our Research on Competition in England's National Health Service', *The Lancet*, 378 (9809), 2064–2065.

Bloom, N., L. Garicano, R. Sadun, and J. Van Reenen, 2014, 'The Distinct Effects of Information Technology and Communication Technology on Firm Organization', *Management Science*, 60 (12), 2859–2885.

Bloom, Nicholas, Charles I. Jones, John Van Reenen, and Michael Webb, 2020, 'Are Ideas Getting Harder to Find?' *American Economic Review*, 110 (4), 1104–1144.

Boeri, T., G. Giupponi, A. Krueger, and S. Machin, 2020, 'Solo Self-Employment and Alternative Work Arrangements: A Cross-Country Perspective on the Changing Composition of Jobs', *Journal of Economic Perspectives*, 34 (1), 170–195.

Borges, J., 1975, 'On Exactitude in Science', in *A Universal History of Infamy*, translated by Norman Thomas de Giovanni, London: Penguin Books, first published in 1946.

Bowles, Samuel, 2004, *Microeconomics: Behavior, Institutions, and Evolution*, Princeton, NJ: Princeton University Press.

Bowles, Samuel, 2016, *The Moral Economy: Why Good Incentives Are No Substitute for Good Citizens*, New Haven, CT: Yale University Press.

Bowles, Samuel, and Wendy Carlin, 2020, 'What Students Learn in Economics 101: Time for a Change', *Journal of Economic Literature*, 58 (1), 176–214.

Britton, Jack, Lorraine Dearden, Laura van der Erve, and Ben Waltmann, 2020, 'The Impact of Undergraduate Degrees on Lifetime Earnings', IFS, https://www.ifs.org.uk/publications/14729.

Browne, Janet, 2003, *Charles Darwin: Voyaging*, London: Pimlico Jonathan Cape, 1995.

Brynjolfsson, Erik, Avinash Collis, and Felix Eggers, 2019, 'Using Massive Online Choice Experiments to Measure Changes in Well-Being', *Proceedings of the National Academy of Sciences*, 116 (15), 7250–7255; doi: 10.1073/pnas.1815663116.

Buchanan, J., and G. Tullock, 1962, *The Calculus of Consent: Logical Foundations of Constitutional Democracy*, Ann Arbor: University of Michigan Press.

Burgin, A., 2012, *The Great Persuasion: Reinventing Free Markets Since the Depression*, Cambridge, MA: Harvard University Press.

Card, David, Stefano DellaVigna, Patricia Funk, and Nagore Iriberri, 2020, 'Are Referees and Editors in Economics Gender-Neutral?, in Shelly Lundberg (ed.), *Women in Economics*, London: VoxEU, 91–96.

Case, A., and A. Deaton, 2020, *Deaths of Despair*, Princeton, NJ: Princeton University Press.

Ceci, Stephen J., Donna K. Ginther, Shulamit Kahn, and Wendy M. Williams, 2014, 'Women in Academic Science: A Changing Landscape', *Psychological Science in the Public Interest*, 15 (3), 75–141.

Cellan-Jones, R., 2021, *Always On*, London: Bloomsbury.

Chan, M. L., 2017, 'The Google Bus', *The Point* (14), July, https://thepointmag.com/examined-life/the-google-bus/, accessed 10 August 2020.

Chen, M. K., V. Lakshminarayanan, and L. Santos, 2005, 'The Evolution of Our Preferences: Evidence from Capuchin Monkey Trading Behaviour', http://www.its.caltech.edu/~camerer/NYU/02-ChenLakshminarayananSantos.pdf.

Christophers, B., 2013, *Banking Across Boundaries*, Hoboken, NJ: Wiley/Blackwell.

Clark, Andrew E., Sarah Flèche, Richard Layard, and Nattavudh Powdthavee, 2018, *The Origins of Happiness: The Science of Well-Being over the Life Course*, Princeton, NJ: Princeton University Press.

Coase, R. H., 1960, 'The Problem of Social Cost', *The Journal of Law and Economics*, 2, 1–44.

Cockshott, P., and D. Zachriah, 2012, 'Arguments for Socialism', http://eprints.gla.ac.uk/58987/.

Colander, D., 2011, 'Creating Humble Economists: A Code of Ethics for Economists' (No. 1103), Middlebury College, Department of Economics.

Colander, D., and R. Kupers, 2014, *Complexity and the Art of Public Policy*, Princeton, NJ: Princeton University Press.

Competition Commission, 2003, 'Extended Warranties on Domestic Electrical Goods: A Report on the Supply of Extended Warranties on Domestic Electrical Goods within the UK', December, https://webarchive.nationalarchives.gov.uk/+/http://www.competition-commission.org.uk//rep_pub/reports/2003/485xwars.htm#full.

Cook, E., 2017, *The Pricing of Progress: Economic Indicators and the Capitalization of American Life*, Cambridge, MA: Harvard University Press.

Corduneanu, Roxana, Adina Dudau, and Georgios Kominis, 2020, 'Crowding-In or Crowding-Out: The Contribution of Self-Determination Theory to Public Service Motivation', *Public Management Review*, 22 (7), 1070–1089, doi: 10.1080/14719037.2020.1740303.

Cottrell, Allin, and W. Paul Cockshott, 1993, 'Calculation, Complexity and Planning: The Socialist Calculation Debate Once Again', http://ricardo.ecn.wfu.edu/~cottrell/socialism_book/calculation_debate.pdf.

Coyle, D., 1997, 1998, *The Weightless World: Strategies for Managing the Digital Economy*, Oxford: Capstone; Cambridge, MA: MIT Press.

Coyle, D., 2007, 2010, *The Soulful Science: What Economists Really Do and Why It Matters*, Princeton, NJ: Princeton University Press.

Coyle, D. (ed.), 2012, *What's The Use of Economics?*, London: London Publishing Partnership.

Coyle, D., 2014, *GDP: A Brief but Affectionate History*, Princeton, NJ: Princeton University Press.

Coyle, D., 2017, 'The Political Economy of National Statistics', in K. Hamilton and C. Hepburn (eds.), *National Wealth: What Is Missing, Why It Matters*, Oxford: Oxford University Press, 15–16.

Coyle, D., 2019a, '*Homo Economicus*, AIs, Humans and Rats: Decision-Making and Economic Welfare', *Journal of Economic Methodology*, 26 (1), 2–12, doi: 10.1080/1350178X.2018.1527135.

Coyle, D., 2019b, 'Practical Competition Policy Tools for Digital Platforms', *Antitrust Law Journal*, 82–83, https://www.americanbar.org/digital-asset-abstract.html/content /dam/aba/publishing/antitrust_law_journal/alj-82-3/ant-coyle.pdf.

Coyle, D., 2020a, 'From Villains to Heroes? The Economics Profession and Its Response to the Pandemic', CEPR Covid Economics, Issue 49, September, 242–256.

Coyle, D., 2020b, *Markets, State and People: Economics for Public Policy*, Princeton, NJ: Princeton University Press.

Coyle, D., 2021, 'Variety and Productivity', Brookings Institute, forthcoming.

Coyle, D., and S. Diepeveen, in progress, 'Creating and Governing Value from Data'.

Coyle, D., S. Diepeveen, J. Tennison, and J. Wdowin, 2020, 'The Value of Data: Policy Implications', Bennett Institute for Public Policy Report, University of Cambridge, Cambridge, UK, https://www.bennettinstitute.cam.ac.uk/publications/value-data -policy-implications/

Coyle, D., and Leonard Nakamura, 2019, 'Towards a Framework for Time Use, Welfare and Household-centric Economic Measurement', ESCoE Working Paper, Economic Statistics Centre of Excellence, London.

Coyle, D., and David Nguyen, 2018, 'Cloud Computing and National Accounting', DP-2018–19, Economic Statistics Centre of Excellence (ESCoE), London.

Coyle, D., and D. Nguyen, 2019, 'Cloud Computing, Cross-Border Data Flows and New Challenges for Measurement in Economics', *National Institute Economic Review*, 249 (1), R30–R38.

Coyle, Diane, and Marianne Sensier, 2020, 'The Imperial Treasury: Appraisal Methodology and Regional Economic Performance in the UK', *Regional Studies*, 54 (3), 283–295, doi: 10.1080/00343404.2019.1606419.

Coyle, D., and A. Weller, 2020, 'What Needs Explaining about AI?' *Science*, 368 (6498), 1433–1434.

Coyle, D., and C. Woolard, 2009, 'Public Value in Practice: Restoring the Ethos of Public Service', BBC Trust, http://downloads.bbc.co.uk/bbctrust/assets/files/pdf /regulatory_framework/pvt/public_value_practice.pdf.

Crémer, J., Y. A. de Montjoye, and H. Schweitzer, 2019, 'Competition Policy for the Digital Era', European Commission, https://ec.europa.eu/competition /publications/reports/kd0419345enn.pdf.

Dasgupta, Partha, 2007, 'Facts and Values in Modern Economics', in H. Kincaid and D. Ross (eds.), *Handbook on the Philosophy of Economic Sciences*, Oxford: Oxford University Press.

David, P. A., 1990, 'The Dynamo and the Computer: An Historical Perspective on the Modern Productivity Paradox', *American Economic Review*, 80 (2), 355–361.

De Waal, F., 2006, *Primates and Philosophers: How Morality Evolved*, Princeton, NJ: Princeton University Press.

Deaton, Angus, 2020, 'Randomization in the Tropics Revisited: A Theme and Eleven Variations', Working Paper No. 27600, National Bureau of Economic Research, Cambridge, MA.

Deringer, W., 2018, *Calculated Values: Finance, Politics, and the Quantitative Age*, Cambridge, MA: Harvard University Press.

Desrosières, A., 2002, *The Politics of Large Numbers: A History of Statistical Reasoning*, Cambridge, MA: Harvard University Press.

Dietz, S., and Cameron Hepburn, 2013, 'Benefit-Cost Analysis of Non-Marginal Climate and Energy Projects', *Energy Economics*, 40 (C), 61–71.

Dinmore, G., 2012, 'Italian Lobbies Apply Brakes to Monti's Reforms', *Financial Times*, 2 January 2012, http://www.ft.com/cms/s/0/fc36edea-3554–11e1–84b9–00144feabdc0.html#axzz1qbX9bJLS, accessed 30 March 2012.

Drèze, J., and Nicholas Stern, 1987, 'The Theory of Cost-Benefit Analysis', in A. J. Auerbach and M. Feldstein (eds.), *Handbook of Public Economics*, Vol. 2, Amsterdam: Elsevier, ch. 14, pp. 909–989.

Ductor, Lorenzo, Sanjeev Goyal, and Anja Prummer, 2020, 'Gender and Collaboration', in Shelly Lundberg (ed.), *Women in Economics*, London: VoxEU, 74–79.

Duflo, Esther, 2017, 'The Economist as Plumber', *American Economic Review*, 107 (5), 1–26.

Earle, Joe, Cahal Moran, and Zach Ward-Perkins, 2016, *The Econonocracy*, Manchester, UK: Manchester University Press.

Easterlin, R., 1974, 'Does Economic Growth Improve the Human Lot? Some Empirical Evidence', in Paul David and Melvin Reader (eds.), *Nations and Households in Economic Growth: Essays in Honor of Moses Abramovitz*, Cambridge, MA: Academic Press.

Easterlin, R., Laura Angelescu McVey, Malgorzata Switek, Onnicha Sawangfa, and Jacqueline Smith Zweig, 2010, 'The Happiness-Income Paradox Revisited', PNAS, December, http://www.pnas.org/content/early/2010/12/08/1015962107.

Enterprise Act 2002, Section 58 and Intervention Order under Section 42 of the Act, October 2008, http://www.legislation.gov.uk/ukpga/2002/40/part/3/chapter/2/.

Epstein, Joshua M., 2007, *Generative Social Science Studies in Agent-Based Computational Modeling*, Princeton, NJ: Princeton University Press.

European Commission, Beyond GDP, http://ec.europa.eu/environment/beyond_gdp/index_en.html.

Evans, David S., and Richard Schmalensee, 2016a, *Matchmakers: The New Economics of Multisided Platforms*, Boston, MA: Harvard Business School Press.

Evans, David S., and Richard Schmalensee, 2016b, 'The New Economics of Multi-Sided Platforms: A Guide to the Vocabulary (9 June), SSRN, https://ssrn.com/abstract=2793021 or http://dx.doi.org/10.2139/ssrn.2793021.

Fanelli, D., 2010, 'Do Pressures to Publish Increase Scientists' Bias? An Empirical Support from US States Data', *PLoS ONE*, 5 (4), e10271, doi:10.1371/journal.pone.0010271.

Fanelli, Daniele, 2018, 'Is Science Really Facing a Reproducibility Crisis?', *Proceedings of the National Academy of Sciences*, 115 (11), 2628–2631, doi: 10.1073/pnas.1708272114.

Farmer, D., and D. Foley, 2009, 'The Economy Needs Agent Based Modelling', *Nature*, 460 (6), 685–686.

Farmer, Roger, 2010, *How the Economy Works: Confidence, Crashes and Self-Fulfilling Prophecies*, Oxford: Oxford University Press.

Fingleton, J., J. Evans, and O. Hogan, 1998, 'The Dublin Taxi Market: Re-regulate or Stay Queuing?', *Studies in Public Policy*, 3, 1–72.

Fitoussi, Jean-Paul, Amartya Sen, and Joseph Stiglitz, 2009, Commission on the Measurement of Economic and Social Progress, 2009, http://ec.europa.eu/eurostat/documents/118025/118123/Fitoussi+Commission+report.

Fourastié, J., 1979, *Les Trente Glorieuses, ou la révolution invisible de 1946 à 1975*, Paris: Fayard.

Fourcade, Marion, Etienne Ollion, and Yann Algan, 2015, 'The Superiority of Economists', *Journal of Economic Perspectives*, 29 (1), 89–114.

Frank, Robert H., Thomas Gilovich, and Dennis T. Regan, 1993, 'Does Studying Economics Inhibit Cooperation?', *Journal of Economic Perspectives*, 7 (2), 159–171.

Frey, C. B., and M. A. Osborne, 2017, 'The Future of Employment: How Susceptible Are Jobs to Computerisation?', *Technological Forecasting and Social Change*, 114, 254–280.

Friedman, M., 1966, 'The Methodology of Positive Economics', in *Essays in Positive Economics*, Chicago: University of Chicago Press, 3–16.

Fryer, R., S. Levitt, J. List, and S. Sadoff, 2012, 'Enhancing the Efficacy of Teacher Incentives through Loss Aversion: A Field Experiment', NBER Working Paper 18237, National Bureau of Economic Research, Cambridge, MA.

Furman, Jason et al., 2019, 'Unlocking Digital Competition', https://assets.publishing.service.gov.uk/government/uploads/system/uploads/attachment_data/file/785547/unlocking_digital_competition_furman_review_web.pdf.

Gallegati, M., and A. Kirman, 2012, 'Reconstructing Economics: Agent Based Models and Complexity', *Complexity Economics*, 1 (1), 5–31.

Gamble, A., 1988, *The Free Economy and the Strong State: The Politics of Thatcherism*, London, New York: Macmillan.

Gawer, A., M. Cusumano, and D. B. Yoffie, 2019, *The Business of Platforms: Strategy in the Age of Digital Competition, Innovation, and Power*, New York: Harper Business, 2019.

Gelman, A., 2013, 'The Recursion of Pop-Econ', Statistical Modeling, Causal Inference, and Social Science, 10 May, https://statmodeling.stat.columbia.edu/2013/05/10/the-recursion-of-pop-econ-or-of-trolling/.

Gerlach, P., 2017, 'The Games Economists Play: Why Economics Students Behave More Selfishly than Other Students', *PloS ONE*, 12 (9), e0183814, https://doi.org/10.1371/journal.pone.0183814.

Gigerenzer, Gerd, 2007, *Gut Feelings: The Intelligence of the Unconscious*, London: Penguin Random House.

Gigerenzer, G., P. M. Todd., and ABC Research Group, 1999, *Simple Heuristics That Make Us Smart*, Oxford: Oxford University Press.

Glaeser, E., and J. A. Scheinkman, 2000, 'Non-market Interactions', NBER Working Paper 8053, National Bureau of Economic Research, Cambridge, MA.

Goodhart, C.A.E., 1975, 'Problems of Monetary Management: The U.K. Experience', Papers in Monetary Economics (1).

Gordon, Robert, 2016, *The Rise and Fall of American Growth: The US Standard of Living Since the Civil War*, Princeton, NJ: Princeton University Press.

Gould, S., 2003, *The Hedgehog, the Fox, and the Magister's Pox*, Cambridge, MA: Harvard University Press.

Graaff, J. de V., 1971, *Theoretical Welfare Economics*, Cambridge: Cambridge University Press, 1971, first published in 1957.

Granovetter, Mark S., 1973, 'The Strength of Weak Ties', *American Journal of Sociology*, 78 (6), 1360–1380.

Griliches, Zvi, 1994, 'Productivity, R&D, and the Data Constraint', *The American Economic Review*, 84 (1), 1–23.

Haldane, A., 2012, 'Towards a Common Financial Language', Bank of England, http://www.bankofengland.co.uk/publications/Pages/speeches/2012/552.aspx, accessed 16 March 2012.

Haldane, A., and R. May, 2011, 'Systemic Risk in Banking Ecosystems', *Nature*, 469, 351–355.

Hall, P. (ed.), 1989, *The Political Power of Economic Ideas*, Princeton, NJ: Princeton University Press.

Hall, P., 1993, 'Policy Paradigms Social Learning, and the State: The Case of Economic Policymaking in Britain', *Comparative Politics*, 25 (3), 275–296, doi:10.2307/422246.

Hall, P. A., and D. Soskice, 2001, *Varieties of Capitalism: The Institutional Foundations of Comparative Advantage*, Oxford: Oxford University Press.

Hammerstein, Peter, and Ronald Noë, 2016, 'Biological Trade and Markets', *Philosophical Transactions of the Royal Society B*, 371, 20150101; doi: 10.1098/rstb.2015.0101.

Hands, David, 2020, *Dark Data*, Princeton, NJ: Princeton University Press.

Harberger, A. C., 1971, 'Three Basic Postulates for Welfare Economics: An Interpretive Essay', *Journal of Economic Literature*, 9 (3), 785–797.

Harris, Robert, 2011, *The Fear Index*, London: Hutchinson.

Haskel, J., and S. Westlake, 2018, *Capitalism without Capital: The Rise of the Intangible Economy*, Princeton, NJ: Princeton University Press.

Hausman, Daniel, and Michael McPherson, 2006, *Economic Analysis, Moral Philosophy and Public Policy*, 2nd ed., Cambridge: Cambridge University Press.

Hausman, Jerry, 2012, 'Contingent Valuation: From Dubious to Hopeless', *Journal of Economic Perspectives*, 26 (4), 43–56.

Hayek, F. A., 1935, 'Socialist Calculation I: The Nature and History of the Problem', reprinted in *Individualism and Economic Order*, 121–147, Chicago: University of Chicago Press, 1948.

Hayek, F., 1944, *The Road to Serfdom*, London: Routledge.

Hayek, F. A., 1945, 'The Use of Knowledge in Society', *The American Economic Review*, 35 (4), 519–530.

Head, M. L., L. Holman, R. Lanfear, A. T. Kahn, and M. D. Jennions, 2015, 'The Extent and Consequences of P-Hacking in Science', *PLoS Biol*, 13 (3), e1002106, https://doi.org/10.1371/journal.pbio.1002106.

Heckman, James J., and Sidharth Moktan, 2020, 'Publishing and Promotion in Economics: The Tyranny of the Top Five', *Journal of Economic Literature*, 58 (2), 419–470.

Hedlund, J., 2000, 'Risky Business: Safety Regulations, Risk Compensation, and Individual Behaviour', *Injury Prevention*, 6, 82–89.

Helpman, E. (ed.), 1998, *General Purpose Technologies and Economic Growth*, Cambridge, MA: MIT Press.

Hengel, Erin, 2020, 'Publishing While Female', in Shelly Lundberg (ed.), *Women in Economics*, London: VoxEU, 80–90.

Herbranson, W., and J. Schroeder, 2010, 'Are Birds Smarter than Mathematicians? Pigeons (*Columba livia*) Perform Optimally on a Version of the Monty Hall Dilemma', *Journal of Comparative Psychology*, 124 (1), 1–13.

Hicks, J., 1937, 'Mr. Keynes and the "Classics"'; A Suggested Interpretation', *Econometrica*, 5 (2), 147–159.

Hicks, J. R., 1939, 'The Foundations of Welfare Economics', *The Economic Journal*, 49 (196), 696–712.

Hicks, J., 1942, *The Social Framework*, Oxford: Clarendon Press.

Hidalgo, C. A., 2021, 'Economic Complexity Theory and Applications', *Nature Review Physics*, 3, 92–113, https://doi.org/10.1038/s42254-020-00275-1.

Hirschman, Daniel, 2016, 'Inventing the Economy Or: How We Learned to Stop Worrying and Love the GDP', PhD dissertation, University of Michigan, Ann Arbor, https://deepblue.lib.umich.edu/handle/2027.42/120713.

HM Treasury, 2003, 'UK Membership of the Single Currency', June 2003, www.hm-treasury.gov.uk/d/EMU03_exec_126.pdf.

HM Treasury, 2011, The Green Book: Appraisal and Evaluation in Central Government, https://www.gov.uk/government/uploads/system/uploads/attachment_data/file/220541/green_book_complete.pdf.

Hoekstra, Mark, Steven L. Puller, and Jeremy West, 2017, 'Cash for Corollas: When Stimulus Reduces Spending', *American Economic Journal: Applied Economics*, 9 (3), 1–35.

Holmstrom, B., and J. Roberts, 1998, 'The Boundaries of the Firm Revisited', *Journal of Economic Perspectives*, 12 (4), 73–94.

Hume, D., 1752, "Essay V. of the Balance of Trade', in *Essays, Moral, Political and Literary*, Part II 'Political Discourses'.

Hurley, S., and M. Nudds, 2006, *Rational Animals?*, Oxford: Oxford University Press.

Hutton, W., 2012, 'Argentina's Oil Grab Is Timely Retort to Rampaging Capitalism', *The Guardian*, 22 April, https://www.theguardian.com/commentisfree/2012/apr/22/will-hutton-argentina-oil-grab-justified.

IDEI, Toulouse School of Economics, 2011, 'The Invisible Hand Meets the Invisible Gorilla: The Economics and Psychology of Scarce Attention', Summary of a conference held at IDEI, Toulouse School of Economics, September, http://www.idei .fr/doc/conf/psy/2011/summary.pdf, accessed 4 May 2012.

Ioannidis, J.P.A., T. D. Stanley, and H. Doucouliagos, 2017, 'The Power of Bias in Economics Research', *The Economic Journal*, 127, F236–F265, doi:10.1111/ecoj.12461.

Johnson, N., G. Zhao, E. Hunsader, J. Meng, A. Ravindar, S. Carran, and B. Tivnan, 2012, 'Financial Black Swans Driven by Ultrafast Machine Ecology', arXiv preprint arXiv:1202.1448.

Johnston, Christopher D., and Andrew O. Ballard, 2016, 'Economists and Public Opinion: Expert Consensus and Economic Policy Judgments', *The Journal of Politics*, 78 (2), 443–456.

Kahneman, D., 2011, *Thinking, Fast and Slow*, New York: Allen Lane.

Kaldor, N., 1939, 'Welfare Propositions of Economics and Interpersonal Comparisons of Utility', *The Economic Journal*, 49 (195), 549–552.

Keim, B., 2012, 'Nanosecond Trading Could Make Markets Go Haywire', *Wired*, 16 February, http://www.wired.com/wiredscience/2012/02/high-speed-trading/all /1, accessed 19 March 2012.

Kelman, S., 1981, 'Cost Benefit Analysis: An Ethical Critique', *Regulation*, 7 February, 33–40.

Kelton, S., 2020, *The Deficit Myth*, London: John Murray.

Keynes, J. M., 1931, 'The Future', in *Essays in Persuasion*, London: Macmillan, 315–334.

Keynes, J. M., 1936, *The General Theory of Employment, Interest and Money*, London: Macmillan.

Khan, Lina M. 2017, 'Amazon's Antitrust Paradox', *Yale Law Journal*, 126 (3), 564–907, https://www.yalelawjournal.org/pdf/e.710.Khan.805_zuvfyyeh.pdf.

Khan, M., 2015, 'UK Economy Grew at Fastest Rate for Nine Years in 2014', *The Telegraph*, 31 March, https://www.telegraph.co.uk/finance/economics/11505763/UK -economy-grew-at-fastest-rate-for-nine-years-in-2014.html.

Klinenberg, Eric, 2002, *Heatwave: A Social Autopsy of Disaster in Chicago*, Chicago: University of Chicago Press.

Kominers, Scott Duke, Alexander Teytelboym, and Vincent P. Crawford, 2017, 'An Invitation to Market Design', *Oxford Review of Economic Policy*, 33 (4), 541–571.

Kondratieff, N., 1935, 'The Long Waves in Economic Life', *The Review of Economics and Statistics*, 17 (6), 105–115.

Korzybski, A., 1933, 'A Non-Aristotelian System and Its Necessity for Rigour in Mathematics and Physics', in *Science and Sanity*, Lakeville, CT: International Non-Aristotelian Library, 747–761.

Krugman, P., 1991, 'Increasing Returns and Economic Geography', *Journal of Political Economy*, 99 (3), 483–499.

Krugman, P., 2006, 'How Did Economists Get It So Wrong?', *New York Times Magazine*, 6 September, http://www.nytimes.com/2009/09/06/magazine/06Economic-t .html?_r=1&pagewanted=all, accessed 30 April 2012.

Kuhn, T., 1996, *The Structure of Scientific Revolutions*, Chicago: University of Chicago Press, first published in 1962.

Lacey, James, 2011, *Keep from All Thoughtful Men: How US Economists Won World War II*, Annapolis, MD: Naval Institute Press.

Lakoff, G., and M. Johnson, 1980, *Metaphors We Live By*, Chicago: University of Chicago Press.

Lanchester, John, 2010, *Whoops!*, London: Penguin.

Lange, O., 1936, 'On the Economic Theory of Socialism', *Review of Economic Studies*, 4 (1), 53–71.

Lange, O., 1937, 'On the Economic Theory of Socialism, Part Two', *Review of Economic Studies*, 4 (2), 123–142.

Lange, O., 1938, 'On the Economic Theory of Socialism,' in B. Lippincott (ed.), *On the Economic Theory of Socialism*, Minneapolis: University of Minnesota Press, 56–143.

Lapuente, V., and S. Van de Walle, 2020, 'The Effects of New Public Management on the Quality of Public Services', *Governance*, 33, 461–475.

Le Grand, J., 1991, 'The Theory of Government Failure', *British Journal of Political Science*, 21 (4), 423–442.

Leamer, E., 1983, 'Let's Take the Con Out of Econometrics', *American Economic Review*, 73 (1), 31–43.

Leamer, E., 2010, 'Tantalus on the Road to Asymptopia', *Journal of Economic Perspectives*, 24 (2), 31–46.

Leibo, Joel Z. , Vinicius Zambaldi, Marc Lanctot, Janusz Marecki, and Thore Graepel, 2017a, 'Multi-Agent Reinforcement Learning in Sequential Social Dilemmas', Cornell University, https://arxiv.org/abs/1702.03037.

Leibo Joel Z., Vinicius Zambaldi, Marc Lanctot, Janusz Marecki, and Thore Graepel, 2017b, 'Multi-Agent Reinforcement Learning in Sequential Social Dilemmas', in S. Das, E. Durfee, K. Larson, M. Winikoff (eds.), Proceedings of the 16th International Conference on Autonomous Agents and Multiagent Systems (AAMAS 2017), Sao Paulo, Brazil, 8–12 May, https://arxiv.org/abs/1702.03037.

Lerner, A., 1938, 'Theory and Practice in Socialist Economics', *Review of Economic Studies*, 6, (1), 71–75.

Little, I.M.D., 1950, *A Critique of Welfare Economics*, Oxford: Clarendon Press.

Lo, A., 2017, *Adaptive Markets: Financial Evolution at the Speed of Thought*, Princeton, NJ: Princeton University Press.

Mackenzie, Donald, 2006, *An Engine, Not a Camera: How Financial Models Shape Markets*, Cambridge, MA: MIT Press.

MacKenzie, D., 2007, 'Option Theory and the Construction of Derivatives Markets', in D. MacKenzie, F. Muniesa, and L. Siu (eds.), *Do Economists Make Markets?*, Princeton, NJ: Princeton University Press, 54–86.

MacKenzie, Donald, 2019, 'Just How Fast?', *London Review of Books*, 41 (5), https://www.lrb.co.uk/the-paper/v41/n05/donald-mackenzie/just-how-fast.

Mance, H., 2016, 'Britain Has Had Enough of Experts, Says Gove', *Financial Times*, 3 June, https://www.ft.com/content/3be49734–29cb-11e6–83e4-abc22d5d108c, accessed 18 October 2018.

Mandel, M., 2012, 'Beyond Goods and Services: The (Unmeasured) Rise of the Data-Driven Economy', Progressive Policy Institute, 10 (October).

Marshall, A., 2013, *Principles of Economics*, London: Palgrave Macmillan, first published in 1890.

Maynard Smith, J., 1976, 'Evolution and the Theory of Games', *American Science*, 64, 41–45.

Maynard Smith, J., and G. R. Price 1973, 'The Logic of Animal Conflict', *Nature*, 246 (5427), 15–18, doi:10.1038/246015a0. S2CID 4224989.

Mazzucato, M., 2013, *The Entrepreneurial State*, London: Anthem Press.

McFadden, D., 1974, 'The Measurement of Urban Travel Demand', *Journal of Public Economics*, 3 (4), 303–328.

Medema, S. G., 2020, ''Exceptional and Unimportant'? Externalities, Competitive Equilibrium, and the Myth of a Pigovian Tradition', *History of Political Economy*, 52 (1), 135–170.

Medina, E., 2011, *Cybernetic Revolutionaries: Technology and Politics in Allende's Chile*, Cambridge, MA: MIT Press.

Merton, R. K., and R. C. Merton, 1968, *Social Theory and Social Structure*, New York: Free Press.

Modestino, Alicia, Pascaline Dupas, Muriel Niederle, and Justin Wolfers, 2020, 'Gender and the Dynamics of Economics Seminars', presentation at American Economic Association Conference, San Diego, CA, USA, 4 January, https://www.aeaweb.org/conference/2020/preliminary/1872.

Mokyr, J., 2017, *A Culture of Growth: The Origins of the Modern Economy*, Princeton, NJ: Princeton University Press.

Moore, A., 2017, *Critical Elitism: Deliberation, Democracy, and the Politics of Expertise*, Cambridge: Cambridge University Press.

Moretti, E., 2012, *The New Geography of Jobs*, Boston: Houghton Mifflin Harcourt.

Morozov, E. 2019, 'Digital Socialism?', *New Left Review*, 116 (March–June), https://newleftreview.org/issues/II116/articles/evgeny-morozov-digital-socialism.

Morson, Gary S., and Morton Schapiro, 2016, *Cents and Sensibility: What Economics Can Learn from the Humanities*, Princeton, NJ: Princeton University Press.

Nordhaus, W. D., 2015, 'Are We Approaching an Economic Singularity? Information Technology and the Future of Economic Growth', NBER Working Paper 21547, National Bureau of Economic Research, Cambridge, MA.

OECD, 2020, 'Better Life Initiative: Measuring Well Being and Progress', http://www.oecd.org/statistics/better-life-initiative.htm.

Olson, M., 1982, *The Rise and Decline of Nations*, New Haven, CT: Yale University Press.

Ormerod, P., 1999, *Butterfly Economics: A New General Theory of Economic and Social Behaviour*, London: Faber and Faber.

Ostrom, E., 1990, *Governing the Commons: The Evolution of Institutions for Collective Action*, Cambridge: Cambridge University Press.

Ottaviano, G., and J. F. Thisse, 2004, 'Agglomeration and Economic Geography', in J. Vernon Henderson and Jacques-François Thisse (eds.), *Handbook of Regional and Urban Economics*, vol. 4, London: Elsevier, 2563–2608.

Oxfam, 2013, 'How to Plan When You Don't Know What Is Going to Happen? Rede-signing Aid for Complex Systems', Oxfam blogs, 14 May, http://www.oxfamblogs .org/fp2p/?p=14588.

Packard, V., 1957, *The Hidden Persuaders*, London: Pelican.

Page, Scott, 2007, *The Difference*, Princeton, NJ: Princeton University Press.

Palley, T., 1997, 'How to Rewrite Economic History', *The Atlantic*, April, https://www .theatlantic.com/magazine/archive/1997/04/how-to-rewrite-economic-history /376830/.

Pastor, L., and P. Veronesi, 2018, Inequality Aversion, Populism, and the Backlash Against Globalization, NBER Working Paper 24900, National Bureau of Economic Research, Cambridge, MA.

Perez, C., 2002, *Technological Revolutions and Financial Capital: The Dynamics of Bubbles and Golden Ages*, London: Elgar.

Pesendorfer, W., 2006, 'Behavioral Economics Comes of Age: A Review Essay on Advances in Behavioral Economics', *Journal of Economic Literature*, 44 (3), 712–721.

Petty, William, 1672, *Essays in Political Arithmetick*.

Philippon, Thomas, 2019, *The Great Reversal: How America Gave Up on Free Markets*, Cambridge, MA: Harvard University Press.

Pigou, A. C., 1908, *Economic Science in Relation to Practice: An Inaugural Lecture Given at Cambridge 30th October, 1908*, London: Macmillan.

Piketty, T., 2014, *Capital in the 21st Century*, Cambridge, MA: Harvard University Press.

Pinker, S., 2007, *The Stuff of Thought: Language as a Window into Human Nature*, London: Penguin.

Pollock, R., 2009, 'Changing the Numbers: UK Directory Enquiries Deregulation and the Failure of Choice', http://rufuspollock.org/2009/02/10/changing-the -numbers-uk-directory-enquiries-deregulation-and-the-failure-of-choice/, accessed 5 April 2012.

Porter, R., 2000, *Enlightenment: Britain and the Creation of the Modern World*, Lon-don: Allen Lane.

Porter, Theodore, 1995, *Trust in Numbers: The Pursuit of Objectivity in Science and Public Life*, Princeton, NJ: Princeton University Press.

Portes, Jonathan, 2012, 'Economists in Government: What Are They Good For?', http://notthetreasuryview.blogspot.co.uk/2012/01/economists-in-government -what-are-they.html, accessed 30 April 2012.

Rawls, J., 1971, *A Theory of Justice*, Cambridge, MA: Harvard University Press.

Reinhart, C., and K. Rogoff, 2009, *This Time Is Different; Eight Centuries of Financial Folly*, Princeton, NJ: Princeton University Press.

Richiardi, M. G., 2016, 'The Future of Agent-Based Modeling', *Eastern Economic Journal*, 43, 271–287, https://doi.org/10.1057/s41302-016-0075-9.

Roberts, K., 1980, 'Price-Independent Welfare Prescriptions', *Journal of Public Eco-nomics*, 13 (3), 277–297.

Roberts, R., 2016, 'When Britain Went Bust: The 1976 IMF Crisis', Official Monetary and Financial Institutions Forum (OMFIF), 28 September.

Robbins, L., 1932, *An Essay on the Nature and Significance of Economic Science*, London: Macmillan.

Robinson, M., 2012, 'Culture after the Credit Crunch', *The Guardian*, 16 March, https://www.theguardian.com/books/2012/mar/16/culture-credit-crunch-marilynne-robinson.

Rodrik, D., 2004, 'Industrial Policy for the Twenty-First Century' (November), Discussion Paper No. 4767, Centre for Economic Policy Research, London.

Rodrik, D., 2013, 'What Is Wrong (and Right) in Economics?', Dani Rodrik's web blog, 7 May, https://rodrik.typepad.com/dani_rodriks_weblog/2013/05/what-is-wrong-and-right-in-economics.html.

Rodrik, D., 2018, 'Is Populism Necessarily Bad Economics?', *AEA Papers & Proceedings*, 108, 196–199.

Rogoff, K., 2019, 'Modern Monetary Nonsense', https://www.project-syndicate.org/commentary/federal-reserve-modern-monetary-theory-dangers-by-kenneth-rogoff-2019-03, accessed 6 August 2020.

Romer, P. M., 1986a, 'Increasing Returns and Long-Run Growth', *Journal of Political Economy*, 94 (5), 1002–1037.

Romer, P. M., 1986b, 'Endogenous Technological Change', *Journal of Political Economy*, 98 (5), S71–S102.

Romer, P., 1994, 'The Origins of Endogenous Growth', *Journal of Economic Perspectives*, 8 (1), 3–22.

Romer, Paul M., 2015, 'Mathiness in the Theory of Economic Growth', *American Economic Review*, 105 (5), 89–93.

Rosen, Sherwin, 1981, 'The Economics of Superstars', *American Economic Review*, 71 (5), 845–858.

Rosenthal, C., 2018, *Accounting for Slavery: Masters and Management*, Cambridge, MA: Harvard University Press.

Roth, A. E., 2002, 'The Economist as Engineer: Game Theory, Experimentation, and Computation as Tools for Design Economics', *Econometrica*, 70 (4), 1341–1378.

Roth, A. E., 2007, 'Repugnance as a Constraint on Markets', *Journal of Economic Perspectives*, 21 (3), 37–58.

Roth, A. E., T. Sönmez, and M.U. Ünver, 2004, 'Kidney Exchange', *The Quarterly Journal of Economics*, 119 (2), 457–488.

Rothschild, E., 2001, *Economic Sentiments: Adam Smith, Condorcet, and the Enlightenment*, Cambridge, MA: Harvard University Press.

Rubinstein, A., 2012, *Economic Fables*, Cambridge, UK: Open Book Publishers.

Ruskin, John, 1860, *Unto This Last*, London: George Allen.

Sahm, Claudia, 2020, 'Economics Is a Disgrace', Macromom blog, https://macromomblog.com/2020/07/29/economics-is-a-disgrace/, accessed 2 August 2020.

Saint-Paul, Gilles, 2011, *The Tyranny of Utility: Behavioral Social Science and the Rise of Paternalism*, Princeton, NJ: Princeton University Press.

Samuelson, P. A., 1983, 'Welfare Economics', in *Foundations of Economic Analysis*, Cambridge, MA: Harvard University Press, first published in 1947, Chapter 9.

Sandel, M. J., 2012, *What Money Can't Buy: The Moral Limits of Markets*, London: Macmillan.

Santos, M. S., and M. Woodford, 1997, 'Rational Asset Pricing Bubbles', *Econometrica*, 65 (1), 19–57.

Satz, D., and J. Ferejohn, 1994, 'Rational Choice and Social Theory', *The Journal of Philosophy*, 91 (2), 71–87.

Schelling, T. C., 1958, 'Design of the Accounts' in *A Critique of the United States Income and Product Accounts*, Princeton, NJ: Princeton University Press for NBER 1958, pp. 325–333, https://www.nber.org/chapters/c0554.pdf, accessed 18 October 2018.

Schelling, T. C., 1960, *The Strategy of Conflict*, Cambridge, MA: Harvard University Press.

Schelling, Thomas, 2006, *Micromotives and Macrobehaviour*, New York: Norton, first published in 1978.

Schmelzer, M., 2016, *The Hegemony of Growth: The OECD and the Making of the Economic Growth Paradigm*, Cambridge: Cambridge University Press.

Schulze, Georg, 2010, *Connectionist Economics*, Bloomington, IN: Trafford Publishing.

Schumpeter, Joseph, 1994, *Capitalism, Socialism and Democracy*, Milton Park, UK: Routledge, first published in 1942.

Scitovszky, T. de, 1941, 'A Note on Welfare Propositions in Economics', *The Review of Economic Studies*, 9 (1), 77–88, https://doi.org/10.2307/2967640.

Scott, J. C., 1998, *Seeing Like a State*, New Haven, CT: Yale University Press.

Scott-Morton, F., et al., 2019, Final Report of Stigler Committee on Digital Platforms, September, https://www.chicagobooth.edu/research/stigler/news-and-media/committee-on-digital-platforms-final-report.

Seabright, P., 2010, *The Company of Strangers: A Natural History of Economic Life*, rev. ed., Princeton, NJ: Princeton University Press.

Segal, D., 2012, 'Is Italy Too Italian?', *New York Times*, 31 July, http://www.nytimes.com/2010/08/01/business/global/01italy.html?pagewanted=all

Sen, A., 1982, *Poverty and Famines: An Essay on Entitlements and Deprivation*, Oxford: Clarendon Press.

Sen, A., 2009, *The Idea of Justice*, London: Allen Lane.

Sen, A., 2017, *Collective Choice and Social Welfare*, London Penguin, expanded edition 2017.

Sen, Amartya, Angus Deaton, and Tim Besley, 2020, 'Economics with a Moral Compass? Welfare Economics: Past, Present, and Future', *Annual Review of Economics*, 12, 1–21.

Sevilla, Almudena, and Sarah Smith, 2020, 'Women in Economics: A UK Perspective', Discussion Paper 15034, Centre for Economic Policy Research, July.

Shapiro, Stuart, 2020, 'OIRA and the Future of Cost-Benefit Analysis', *The Regulatory Review*, https://www.theregreview.org/2020/05/19/shapiro-oira-future-cost-benefit-analysis/

Shearer, J. C., J. Abelson, B. Kouyaté, J. N. Lavis, and G. Walt, 2016, 'Why Do Policies Change? Institutions, Interests, Ideas and Networks in Three Cases of Policy Reform', *Health Policy and Planning*, 31 (9), 1200–1211.

Shiller, R., 2000, *Irrational Exuberance*, Princeton, NJ: Princeton University Press.

Shiller, R., 2003, *The New Financial Order: Risk in the 21st Century*, Princeton, NJ: Princeton University Press.

Shiller, R., 2013, *Finance and the Good Society*, Princeton, NJ: Princeton University Press.

Shiller, Robert J., 2017, 'Narrative Economics', *American Economic Review*, 107 (4), 967–1004, doi: 10.1257/aer.107.4.967.

Shiller, R. J., 2019, *Narrative Economics: How Stories Go Viral and Drive Major Economic Events*, Princeton, NJ: Princeton University Press.

Silver, N., 2012, *The Signal and the Noise: The Art and Science of Prediction*, London: Penguin.

Skidelsky, R., 1992, *John Maynard Keynes: A Biography*, Vol. 2: *The Economist as Saviour*, 1920–1937, London: Macmillan.

Skidelsky, Robert, 2020, *What's Wrong with Economics: A Primer for the Perplexed*, New Haven, CT: Yale University Press.

Slobodian, Quinn, 2018, *Globalists: The End of Empire*, Cambridge, MA: Harvard University Press.

Smith, A., 2000, *The Theory of Moral Sentiments,* New York: Prometheus Books, first published in 1759.

Smith, G., 2012, 'Why I Am Leaving Goldman Sachs', *New York Times*, 14 March, http://www.nytimes.com/2012/03/14/opinion/why-i-am-leaving-goldman-sachs .htm?pagewanted=1&_r=1, accessed 14 March 2012.

Snider, J., 2011, 'Finance Now Exists for Its Own Exclusive Benefit', Real Clear Markets, http://www.realclearmarkets.com/articles/2011/12/16/finance_now_exists_for _its_own_exclusive_benefit_99422.html, accessed 24 April 2012.

Snow, C. P., 1963. *The Rede Lecture: The Two Cultures,* Cambridge: Cambridge University Press, first published in 1959.

Solnit, R., 2014, 'Get Off the Bus', *London Review of Books*, 36 (4), https://www.lrb.co .uk/the-paper/v36/n04/rebecca-solnit/diary, accessed 10 August 2020.

Solow, Robert, 1987, 'We'd Better Watch Out', *New York Times Book Review*, 12 July, 36.

Spufford, F., 2010, *Red Plenty*, London: Faber and Faber.

Spulber, D. F., 2019, 'The Economics of Markets and Platforms', *Journal of Economics & Management Strategy*, 28, 159–172.

Stanovich, K. E., 2005, *The Robot's Rebellion: Finding Meaning in the Age of Darwin*, Chicago: University of Chicago Press.

Stapleford, T. A., 2009, *The Cost of Living in America*, Cambridge: Cambridge University Press.

Stedman Jones, Daniel, 2012, *Masters of the Universe*, Princeton, NJ: Princeton University Press.

Steil, B., 2018, *The Marshall Plan: Dawn of the Cold War*, Oxford: Oxford University Press.

Stern, N., 2007. 'The Economics of Climate Change', https://webarchive.nationalarchives
.gov.uk/20070222000000/http://www.hmtreasury.gov.uk/independent_reviews
/stern_review_economics_climate_change/stern_review_report.html, accessed 10
August 2020.

Stevenson, B., and J. Wolfers, 2008, 'Economic Growth and Subjective Well-Being:
Reassessing the Easterlin Paradox', Brookings Papers on Economic Activity,
Spring.

Stiglitz, Joseph E., with Bruce C. Greenwald, 2014, *Creating a Learning Society: A
New Approach to Growth, Development, and Social Progress*, New York: Columbia
University Press.

Storper, M., and R. Salais, 1997, *Worlds of Production: The Action Frameworks*, Cambridge, MA: Harvard University Press.

Sugden, R., 2018, *The Community of Interest*, Oxford: Oxford University Press.

Sugden, R., 2020, 'Normative Economics Without Preferences', *International Review
of Economics*, online 23 July 2020.

Sundararajan, A., 2016, *The Sharing Economy: The End of Employment and the Rise of
Crowd-Based Capitalism*, Cambridge, MA: MIT Press.

Sunstein, Cass R., 2003, 'Libertarian Paternalism', *American Economic Review*, 93 (2),
175–179.

Sutton, J., 2000, *Marshall's Tendencies: What Can Economists Know?*, London: MIT
Press and Leuven University Press.

Takagi, S., 2020, 'Literature Survey on the Economic Impact of Digital Platforms',
International Journal of Economic Policy Studies, 14, 449–464, https://doi.org/10
.1007/s42495-020-00043-0.

Tassey, Gregory, 2014, 'Competing in Advanced Manufacturing: The Need for Improved
Growth Models and Policies', *Journal of Economic Perspectives*, 28 (1), 27–48.

Taylor, P., 2013, 'Sennheiser Fights Fake Electronic Goods', *Financial Times*, 12 May,
https://www.ft.com/content/6454afe8-b9a7-11e2-9a9f-00144feabdc0.

Thoma, M., 2011, 'New Forms of Communication and the Public Mission of Economics: Overcoming the Great Disconnect', November, http://publicsphere.ssrc.org
/thoma-new-forms-of-communication-and-the-public-mission-of-economics/,
accessed 27 March 2012.

Tirole, J., 1988, *Theory of Industrial Organization*, Cambridge, MA: MIT Press.

Tirole, Jean, 2016, *Economie du bien commun*, Paris, France: PUF.

Tooze, Adam, 2001, *Statistics and the German State 1900–1945: The Making of Modern
Economic Knowledge*, Cambridge: Cambridge University Press.

Triennial Central Bank Survey of Foreign Exchange and Derivatives Market Activity
in 2010—Final results, 2010, https://www.bis.org/publ/rpfxf10t.htm.

Tucker, Paul, 2019, *Unelected Power*, Princeton, NJ: Princeton University Press.

Turner, A., 2010, 'After the Crises: Assessing the Costs and Benefits of Financial
Liberalisation', Speech by Lord Adair Turner, Chairman, UK Financial Services
Authority, at the Fourteenth C. D. Deshmukh Memorial Lecture on 15 February,
Mumbai.

Van Doren, P., 2021, 'GameStop, Payments for Order Flow, and High Frequency Trading', Cato Institute, 1 February, https://www.cato.org/blog/gamestop-payments-order-flow-high-frequency-trading, accessed 6 February 2021.

Van Reenen, J., 2018, 'Increasing Differences Between Firms: Market Power and the Macro-Economy,' CEP Discussion Papers 1576, Centre for Economic Performance, London School of Economics.

Vaughan, N., 2020, *The Flash Crash,* New York: Penguin Random House.

Von Mises, L., 1920, 'Die Wirtschaftsrechnung im sozialistischen Gemeinwesen', *Archiv für Sozialwissenschaften,* 47, 186–121; published in English as "Economic Calculation in the Socialist Commonwealth", trans. S. Adler, in F. A. Hayek (ed.), *Collectivist Economic Planning: Critical Studies on the Possibilities of Socialism,* London: Routledge & Kegan Paul Ltd., 1935, ch. 3, 87–130.

Waldrop, M. M., 2001, *The Dream Machine: JCR Licklider and the Revolution That Made Computing Personal,* London: Viking Penguin.

Williams, E., and Coase, R., 1964, 'The Regulated Industries: Discussion', *The American Economic Review,* 54 (3), Papers and Proceedings of the Seventy-sixth Annual Meeting of the American Economic Association (May 1964), 192–197.

Wren-Lewis, S., 2012a, 'Microfoundations and Central Bank Models', Mainly Macro Blog, 26 March, http://mainlymacro.blogspot.co.uk/2012/03/microfoundations-and-central-bank.html.

Wren-Lewis, S., 2012b, 'The Return of Schools of Thought', http://mainlymacro.blogspot.co.uk/2012/01/return-of-schools-of-thought-macro.html, accessed 24 April 2012.

Wu, Alice H., 2018, 'Gendered Language on the Economics Job Market Rumors Forum', *AEA Papers and Proceedings,* 108, 175–179.

Wu, T., 2016, *The Attention Merchants,* New York: Knopf.

YouGov, 2011, 'Wanted: A Better Capitalism', 16 May, http://labs.yougov.co.uk/news/2011/05/16/wanted-better-capitalism/.

Young, A., 2017, 'Consistency without Inference: Instrumental Variables', LSE Working Paper, London School of Economics, http://personal.lse.ac.uk/YoungA/CWOI.pdf, accessed 6 August 2020.

Ziliak, S., and D. N. McCloskey, 2008, *The Cult of Statistical Significance: How the Standard Error Costs Us Jobs, Justice, and Lives,* Ann Arbor: University of Michigan Press.

INDEX

Page references in *italics* indicate a table or figure.

73; macroeconomics and, 17, 21, 31,
36–37, 71–76, 85–86; market as process and, 37–45; political economy
and, 11, 49, 56, 70–80, 82; politics
and, 29, 33, 36, 41, 53, 55–56, 61,
64–73, 76–79, 85; putting economists into economics and, 61–66;
rationality and, 15–16, 20–22, 29,
31, 33, 35, 45–48, 54, 59, 62–63, 71;
regulation and, 16, 19, 24–32, 39,
41, 43, 53, 57–71, 81; responsible
economics and, 52–61; statistics
and, 17, 42, 51–52, 58, 61, 72, 90,
94–102, 113; technocratic dilemma
and, 67–79; technology and, 26–28,
35, 40, 71; welfare and, 55, 60

randomised control trials (RCTs),
60–61, 93–95, 105, 109–10
rational choice theory, 33, 35, 47–48,
59, 91, 114, 119
rationality: algorithms and, 116, 118;
artificial intelligence (AI) and,
116–18; behavioural economics and,
22, 35, 46–47, 59, 109, 117–19; common sense and, 78, 127; competition
and, 117; computers and, 116–17;
consumers and, 116; decision making and, 116–19; empirical work and,
17; Enlightenment and, 20; game
theory and, 48, 90–91, 129, 159–60,
179–80; happiness and, 70–71, 153;
homo economicus and, 13, 47–48,
93, 114, 116–17; logical rigour and,
88; logic and, 33, 47, 89–91; models
and, 21–22, 31, 35, 45–48, 62, 71,
88–103, 117–18; moral issues and,
117; New Public Management and,
33, 106–7, 119, 187; outsider context
and, 90–93, 109, 111; political economy and, 119; progress and, 157;
public responsibilities and, 15–16,
20–22, 29, 31, 33, 35, 45–48, 54, 59,
62–63, 71; self-interest and, 6, 13,
46–47, 109, 117–20, 123; separation
protocol and, 123–24; twenty-first-
century policy and, 194

Rawls, John, 106
Reagan, Ronald, 15–16, 30–31, 36,
56–57, 124, 192–94, 207
RealClear Opinion, 19
recession, 17, 51, 73, 111, 154, 158–59
reciprocity, 49
Red Plenty (Spufford), 182–83, 190
Rees-Mogg, Jacob, 155
reflexivity, 11, 81
reform, 4–5, 34, 44–45, 67–69, 88, 172
regulation: Big Bang and, 16; deregulation and, 16, 31, 60, 68, 71, 193–94;
greed and, 11; Market Abuse Regulation (MAR) and, 27n5; outsider
context and, 109; price gouging
and, 43; progress and, 149, 156–58,
165; public responsibilities and, 16,
19, 24–32, 39, 41, 43, 53, 57–71, 81;
separation protocol and, 125; technology and, 27, 71, 134, 181; twenty-
first-century policy and, 193–94, 200,
206; utilities and, 65
Reinhart, Carmen, 101
Renaissance, 144
rent-seeking, 64
Republic of Beliefs, The (Basu), 159–60
Retail Price Index (RPI), 147
Rethinking Economics group, 35, 84
returns to scale: envelopment and,
203–4; increasing, 123, 128, 140,
174, 177, 180, 185–88, 199, 202–3,
209; knowledge-based economy
and, 128; production and, 123, 128,
140, 174, 177, 180, 185–88, 199, 202–3,
209; progress and, 140; twenty-first-
century policy and, 185–88, 199,
202–3, 209
Robbins, Lionel, 100, 120–21
Roberts, J., 197
Robinhood, 27
Robinson, Marilynne, 19–20
robotics, 137, 154
Rodrik, Dani, 97
Rogoff, Ken, 101
Romer, Paul, 90, 140, 209
Rosen, Sherwin, 173–74
Ross, Andy, 83–84